THE MYSTICAL HYMNS OF ORPHEUS

THE MYSTICAL HYMNS OF ORPHEUS

THOMAS TAYLOR

Athens ✠ Manchester

The Mystical Hymns of Orpheus

Published by: Old Book Publishing Ltd

Book Cover Design: Old Book Publishing Ltd

Copyright © 2012 Old Book Publishing Ltd
All rights reserved.

Title of original: The Mystical Hymns of Orpheus
Originally published in 1787

Cover image: Orpheus with the lyre and surrounded by beasts, *(Byzantine & Christian Museum, Athens).*

ISBN–10: 1-78107-138-1
ISBN–13: 978-1-78107-138-0

EDITOR'S NOTE

Old Book Publishing Ltd takes care in preserving the wording and images of the original books. For this reason we have invested in technology that enables us to enhance the quality of such reproduction. This investment helps overcome problems encountered when reproducing old books, such as stains, coloured paper, discolouration of ink, yellowed pages, see-through and onion skin type paper.

This reproduction book, produced from digital images of the original, may contain occasional defects such as missing pages or blemishes due to the original source content or were introduced by the scanning process.

These are scanned pages and the quality of print represents accurately the print quality of the original book, though we may have been able to enhance it.

As this book has been scanned and/or reformatted from the original we cannot guarantee that it is error-free or contains the full content of the original.

However, we believe that this work is culturally important, and despite its imperfections, have elected to bring it back into print as part of our commitment to the preservation of printed works.

Old Book Publishing

THE
MYSTICAL HYMNS

OF

ORPHEUS.

TRANSLATED FROM THE GREEK,

AND DEMONSTRATED TO BE THE

Invocations which were used in the Eleusinian Mysteries,

BY THOMAS TAYLOR.

Φθεγξομαι οις θεμις εστι, θυρας δ' επιθεσθε βεβηλοι
Παντις ομως. ORPHEUS.

The Second Edition.

WITH CONSIDERABLE
EMENDATIONS, ALTERATIONS, AND ADDITIONS.

CHISWICK:
Printed by C. Whittingham,
COLLEGE HOUSE;

FOR THE TRANSLATOR, MANOR PLACE, WALWORTH;

AND SOLD

BY ROBERT TRIPHOOK, 23, OLD BOND STREET.

1824.

TO

PRINCE AUGUSTUS FREDERICK,

DUKE OF SUSSEX,

K. G. D.C.L. ETC. ETC. ETC. ETC.

AS A TESTIMONY

OF THE GREATEST RESPECT FOR HIS PRIVATE AND
PUBLIC VIRTUES,

AND HIS

VERY SUPERIOR LITERARY ATTAINMENTS,

WHICH GIVE AN ADDITIONAL DIGNITY AND SPLENDOUR

TO ROYALTY ITSELF,

THIS WORK IS INSCRIBED

BY HIS MOST DEVOTED AND OBEDIENT SERVANT,

THE TRANSLATOR,

THOMAS TAYLOR.

INTRODUCTION.

The Grecian theology, which originated from Orpheus, was not only promulgated by him, but also by Pythagoras and Plato; who, for their transcendent genius, will always be ranked by the intelligent among the prodigies of the human race. By the first of these illustrious men, however, it was promulgated mystically and symbolically; by the second, enigmatically, and through images; and scientifically by the third. That this theology, indeed, was derived from Orpheus is clearly testified by those two great philosophic luminaries Iamblichus[1] and Proclus[2]. For by

---

[1] περι θεων Πυθαγορας ο τω Μνησαρχω τουτο εξεμαθον, οργιασθεις εν Λιβηθροις τοις Θρᾳκιοις Αγλαοφαμω τελετας μεταδοντος· ως αρα Ορφευς ο Καλλιοπας κατα το Παγγαιον ορος υπο τας ματρος πινυσθεις εφα ταν αριθμω ουσιαν αἰδιον ειναι. Iamblicus de Vit. Pythag. p. 135.

[2] Πυθαγορειος ο Τιμαιος επεται ταις Πυθαγορειων αρχαις, αυται δε εισιν αι Ορφικαι παραδοσεις· α γαρ Ορφευς δι' απορ-

them we are informed, " that what Orpheus delivered mystically through arcane narrations, this Pythagoras learned when he celebrated orgies in the Thracian Libethra, being initiated by Aglaophemus in the mystic wisdom which Orpheus derived from his mother Calliope, in the mountain Pangæus."

This sublime theology, though it was scientifically disseminated by Plato, yet conformably to the custom of the most ancient philosophers, was delivered by him synoptically, and in such a way as to be inaccessible to the vulgar; but when, in consequence of the commencement of a degraded and barren period, this theology became corrupted through the negligence and confusion of its votaries, then such of his disciples as happened to live when it was thus degraded and deformed found it necessary to unfold it more fully, in order to prevent its becoming utterly extinct. The men by whom this arduous task was accomplished were the last of the disciples of Plato; men who, though they lived in a base

---

ρητων λογων μυστικως παραδεδωκε, ταυτα Πυθαγορας εξεμαθεν οργιασθεις εν Λιβηθροις τοις Θρακιοις, Αγλιοφαμου τελετας μεταδιδοντος, ην περι θεων σοφιαν παρα Καλλιοπης της μητρος επινυσθη. Proclus in Tim. lib. v. p. 291.

INTRODUCTION.

age, possessed a divine genius, and who having happily fathomed the depth of their great master's works, luminously and copiously developed their recondite meaning, and benevolently communicated it in their writings for the general good.

From this golden chain of philosophers, as they have been justly called, my elucidations of the present mystic hymns are principally derived: for I know of no other genuine sources, if it be admitted (and it must by every intelligent reader), that the theology of Orpheus is the same as that of Pythagoras and Plato. Hence I shall not take any notice of the theories of Bryant and Faber and other modern mythological writers; because these theories, however ingenious they may be, are so far from elucidating, that they darken, confound, and pollute the Grecian theology, by mingling with it other systems, to which it is as perfectly foreign and hostile as wisdom is to folly, and intellect to craft.

That the philosophic reader therefore may be convinced of the truth of this observation, the following epitome of this theology, derived from the abovementioned sources, is subjoined. In the first place, this theology celebrates the immense principle of things as something superior even to being itself; as exempt from the whole of things, of which it is nevertheless ineffably the source; and does not therefore think fit to connumerate it with any triad, or order of beings. Indeed, it even apologizes for attempting to give an appropriate name to this principle, which is in reality ineffable, and ascribes the attempt to the imbecility of human nature, which striving intently to behold it, gives the appellation of the most simple of its conceptions to that which is beyond all knowledge and all conception. Hence Plato denominates it *the one* and *the good;* by the former of these names indicating its transcendent simplicity, and by the latter its subsistence as the object of desire to all beings. For all things desire good. But Orpheus, as Proclus well observes[3], " availing himself of the license of fables, manifests every thing prior to Heaven (or the intelligible and at the same time intellectual order) by names, as far as to the first cause. He also denominates the ineffable, who transcends the intelligible unities, Time." And this according to a wonderful analogy, indicating the *generation,* i. e. the

[3] In. Plat. Cratyl. p. 23.

INTRODUCTION. xi

ineffable evolution into light of all things, from the immense principle of all. For, as Proclus elsewhere observes, " where there is *generation* there also time has a subsistence." And in this way the celebrated *Theogony* of Orpheus and other Grecian theologists is to be understood.

As the first cause then is *the one*, and this is the same with *the good*, the universality of things must form a whole, the best and the most profoundly united in all its parts which can possibly be conceived: for *the first good* must be the cause of the greatest good, that is, the whole of things; and as goodness is union, the best production must be that which is most united. But as there is a difference in things, and some are more excellent than others, and this in proportion to their proximity to the first cause, a profound union can no otherwise take place than by the extremity of a superior order coalescing through intimate alliance with the summit of one proximately inferior. Hence the first of bodies, though they are essentially corporeal, yet κατα σχεσιν, through *habitude* or *alliance*, are most vital, or lives. The highest of souls are after this manner intellects, and the first of beings are Gods. For as *being* is the highest of things after *the first cause*, its first subsistence must be according to a superessential characteristic.

Now that which is superessential, considered as participated by the highest or *true being*, constitutes that which is called *intelligible*. So that every true being depending on the Gods is a *divine intelligible*. It is *divine* indeed, as that which is deified; but it is *intelligible*, as the object of desire to intellect, as perfective and connective of its nature, and as the plenitude of *being* itself. But in the first being life and intellect subsist according to cause: for every thing subsists either according to *cause*, or according to *hyparxis*, or according to *participation*. That is, every thing may be considered either as subsisting occultly in its cause, or openly in its own order (or according to what it is), or as participated by something else. The first of these is analogous to light when viewed subsisting in its fountain the sun; the second to the light immediately proceeding from the sun; and the third to the splendour communicated to other natures by this light.

The first procession therefore from the first cause will be the intelligible triad, consisting of *being*, *life*, and *intellect*, which are the three

INTRODUCTION. xiii

highest things after the first God, and of which *being* is prior to *life*, and *life* to *intellect*. For whatever partakes of life partakes also of being: but the contrary is not true, and therefore being is above life; since it is the characteristic of higher natures to extend their communications beyond such as are subordinate. But *life* is prior to *intellect*, because all intellectual natures are vital, but all vital natures are not intellectual. But in this intelligible triad, on account of its superessential characteristic, all things may be considered as subsisting according to cause: and consequently number here has not a proper subsistence, but is involved in unproceeding union, and absorbed in superessential light. Hence, when it is called a triad, we must not suppose that any *essential distinction* takes place, but must consider this appellation as expressive of its ineffable perfection. For as it is the nearest of all things to *the one*, its union must be transcendently profound and ineffably occult.

All the Gods indeed, considered according to their unities, are all in all, and are at the same time united with the first God, like rays to light, or the radii of a circle to the centre. And hence they are all established in their ineffable principle (as Proclus in Parmenid. beautifully observes), like the roots of trees in the earth; so that they are all as much as possible superessential, just as trees are eminently of an earthly nature, without at the same time being earth itself. For the nature of the earth, as being a whole, and therefore having a perpetual subsistence, is superior to the partial natures which it produces. The intelligible triad therefore, from existing wholly according to the superessential, possesses an inconceivable profundity of union both with itself and its cause; and hence it appears to the eye of intellect as one simple indivisible splendour, beaming from an unknown and inaccessible fire.

The Orphic theology, however, concerning the intelligible Gods, or the highest order of divinities, is, as we are informed by Damascius[4], as follows: " *Time* [as we have already observed] is symbolically said to be the one principle of the universe; but *ether* and *chaos*[5] are celebrated as the two principles immediately posterior to this one. And *being*,

---

[4] Vid. Wolfii Anecdot. Græc. tom. iii. p. 252.

[5] These two principles are called by Plato, in the Philebus, *bound* and *infinity*.

simply considered, is represented under the symbol of an *egg*[6]. And this is the first triad of the intelligible Gods. But for the perfection of the second triad they establish either a conceiving and a conceived egg as a God, or a white garment, or a cloud: because from these Phanes leaps forth into light. For indeed they philosophize variously concerning the middle triad. But Phanes here represents intellect. To conceive him however besides this, as father and power, contributes nothing to Orpheus. But they call the third triad Metis as *intellect*[7], Ericapæus as *power*, and Phanes as *father*. But sometimes[8] the middle triad is considered according to the three-shaped God, while conceived in the egg: for the middle always represents each of the extremes; as in this instance, where the egg and the three-shaped God subsist together. And here you may perceive that the egg is that which is united; but that the

---

[6] This Orphic *egg* is the same with the *mixture* from *bound* and *infinity*, mentioned by Plato in the Philebus. See the third book of my translation of Proclus on the Theology of Plato.

[7] ως νουν is omitted in the original.

[8] μηποτε is erroneously printed instead of ποτε.

three-shaped and really multiform God is the separating and discriminating cause of that which is intelligible. Likewise the middle triad subsists according to the egg, as yet united; but the third[9] according to the God who separates and distributes the whole intelligible order. And this is the common and familiar Orphic theology. But that delivered by Hieronymus and Hellanicus is as follows. According to them *water* and *matter* were the first productions, from which earth was secretly drawn forth: so that water and earth are established as the two first principles; the latter of these having a *dispersed* subsistence; but the former conglutinating and connecting the latter. They are silent however concerning the principle prior to these two, as being ineffable: for as there are no illuminations about him, his arcane and ineffable nature is from hence sufficiently evinced. But the third principle posterior to these two, *water* and *earth*, and which is generated from them, is *a dragon*, naturally endued with the heads of a bull and a lion, but in the middle having the countenance of

---

[9] το τριτον is I conceive erroneously omitted in the original.

the God himself. They add likewise that he has wings on his shoulders, and that he is called *undecaying Time*, and *Hercules;* that *Necessity* resides with him, which is the same as *Nature*, and incorporeal *Adrastia*, which is extended throughout the universe, whose limits she binds in amicable conjunction. But as it appears to me, they denominate this third principle as established according to essence; and assert, besides this, that it subsists as male and female, for the purpose of exhibiting the generative causes of all things.

"I likewise find in the Orphic rhapsodies, that neglecting the two first principles, together with the one principle who is delivered in silence, the third principle, posterior to the two, is established by the theology as the original; because this first of all possesses something effable and commensurate to human discourse. For in the former hypothesis, the highly reverenced and undecaying *Time*, the father of æther and chaos, was the principle: but in this *Time* is neglected, and the principle becomes *a dragon*. It likewise calls triple æther, moist; and chaos, infinite; and Erebus, cloudy and dark; delivering this second triad analogous to the first: this being potential, as that was paternal. Hence the third procession of this triad is dark Erebus: its paternal and summit æther, not according to a simple but intellectual subsistence: but its middle infinite chaos, considered as a progeny or procession, and among these parturient, because from these the third intelligible triad proceeds. What then is the third intelligible triad? I answer, the egg; the duad of the natures of male and female which it contains, and the multitude of all-various seeds, residing in the middle of this triad: And the third among these is an incorporeal God, bearing golden wings on his shoulders; but in his inward parts naturally possessing the heads of bulls, upon which heads a mighty dragon appears, invested with the all-various forms of wild beasts. This last then must be considered as the *intellect* of the triad; but the middle progeny, which are *many* as well as *two*, correspond to *power*, and the egg itself is *the paternal principle* of the third triad: but the third God of this third triad, this theology celebrates as *Protogonus*, and calls him *Jupiter*, the disposer of all things and of the whole world; and on this account denominates him *Pan*. And such is the information which this theology affords us, concerning the genealogy of the intelligible principles of things.

But in the writings of the Peripatetic Eudemus, containing the theology of Orpheus, the whole intelligible order is passed over in silence, as being every way ineffable and unknown, and incapable of verbal enunciation. Eudemus therefore commences his genealogy from *Night*, from which also Homer begins: though Eudemus is far from making the Homeric genealogy consistent and connected, for he asserts that Homer begins from Ocean and Tethys. It is however apparent, that *Night* is according to Homer the greatest divinity, since she is reverenced even by Jupiter himself. For the poet says of Jupiter, " that he feared lest he should act in a manner displeasing to swift *Night*[10]." So that Homer begins his genealogy of the Gods from *Night*. But it appears to me that Hesiod, when he asserts that Chaos was first generated, signifies by Chaos the incomprehensible and perfectly united nature of that

---

[10] ἅζετο γὰρ μὴ νυκτὶ θοῇ ἀπόθύμια ῥέζοι. So Damascius; but instead of ῥέζοι, all the printed editions of Homer read ἔρδοι.

xx INTRODUCTION.

which is intelligible: but that he produces Earth[11] the first from thence, as a certain principle of the whole procession of the Gods. Unless perhaps Chaos is the second of the two principles: but Earth[12], Tartarus, and Love form the triple intelligible. So that *Love* is to be placed for the third monad of

[11] Την is printed instead of Γην.

[12] As the whole of the Grecian theology is the progeny of the mystic traditions of Orpheus, it is evident that the Gods which Hesiod celebrates by the epithets of *Earth, Heaven*, &c. cannot be the visible *Heaven* and *Earth:* for Plato in the Cratylus, following the Orphic doctrine concerning the Gods, as we have evinced in our notes on that dialogue, plainly shows, in explaining the name of Jupiter, that this divinity is the artificer of the sensible universe; and consequently *Saturn, Heaven, Earth*, &c. are much superior to the mundane deities. Indeed if this be not admitted, the Theogony of Hesiod must be perfectly absurd and inexplicable. For why does he call Jupiter, agreeably to Homer, (πατηρ ανδρων τε θεων τε), "*father of gods and men?*" Shall we say that he means literally that Jupiter is the father of *all* the Gods? But this is impossible; for he delivers the generation of Gods who are the parents of Jupiter. He can therefore only mean that Jupiter is the parent of all the mundane Gods: and his Theogony, when considered according to this exposition, will be found to be beautifully consistent and sublime; whereas, according to modern interpretations, the whole is a mere chaos, more wild than the delirious visions of Swendenborg, and more unconnected than any of the impious effusions of methodistical rant. I only add, that την is again erroneously printed in the Excerpta of Wolfius for γην.

the intelligible order, considered according to its convertive nature; for it is thus denominated by Orpheus in his rhapsodies. But *Earth* for the first, as being first established in a certain firm and essential station. But *Tartarus* for the middle, as in a certain respect exciting and moving forms into distribution. But Acusilaus appears to me to establish *Chaos* for the first principle, as entirely unknown; and after this, two principles, *Erebus* as male, and *Night* as female; placing the latter for *infinity*, but the former for *bound*. But from the mixture of these, he says[13] that *Æther*, *Love*, and *Counsel* are generated, forming three intelligible hypostases. And he places *Æther* as the summit; but *Love* in the middle, according to its naturally middle subsistence; but *Metis* or *Counsel* as the third, and the same as highly reverenced intellect. And, according to the history of Eudemus, from these he produces a great number of other Gods.

Thus far Damascius, with whose very interesting narration the doctrine of the Chaldeans concerning the intelligible order accords, as delivered by Johannes Picus in his

---

[13] φημμ in the original should doubtless be φησι.

Conclusions according to the Opinion of the Chaldean Theologists[14]. "The intelligible coordination (says he) is not in the intellectual coordination, as Amasis the Egyptian asserts, but is above every intellectual hierarchy, imparticipably concealed in the abyss of the first unity, and under the obscurity of the first darkness." Coordinatio intelligibilis non est in intellectuali coordinatione, ut dixit Amasis Ægyptius, sed est super omnem intellectualem hierarchium, in abysso primæ unitatis, et sub caligine primarum tenebrarum imparticipaliter abscondita.

But from this triad it may be demonstrated, that all the processions of the Gods may be comprehended in six orders, viz. the *intelligible order*, the *intelligible and at the same time intellectual*, the *intellectual*, the *supermundane*, the *liberated*, and the *mundane*[15]. For the *intelligible*, as we have already observed, must hold the first rank, and must consist of *being, life*, and *intellect*; i. e. must *abide, proceed*, and *return*; at the same time that it is characterized, or subsists principally according to

---

[14] Vid. Pici Opera, tom. i. p. 54.

[15] i. e. θεοι νοητοι, νοητοι και νοεροι, νοεροι, υπερκοσμιοι, απολυτοι sive υπερουρανιοι, et εγκοσμιοι.

causally *permanent being*. But in the next place, that which is both *intelligible* and *intellectual* succeeds, which must likewise be triple, but must principally subsist according to *life*, or *intelligence*. And in the third place the *intellectual* order must succeed, which is *triply convertive*. But as in consequence of the existence of the sensible world, it is necessary that there should be some demiurgic cause of its existence, this cause can only be found in *intellect*, and in the last hypostasis of the *intellectual triad*. For all forms in this hypostasis subsist according to all-various and perfect divisions; and forms can only fabricate when they have a perfect intellectual separation from each other. But since *fabrication* is nothing more than *procession*, the Demiurgus will be to the posterior orders of Gods what *the one* is to the orders prior to the *Demiurgus;* and consequently he will be that secondarily which the first cause of all is primarily. Hence his first production will be an order of Gods analogous to the *intelligible* order, and which is denominated *supermundane*. After this he must produce an order of Gods similar to the *intelligible* and *intellectual* order, and which are denominated *liberated* Gods. And in the last place, a procession correspondent to the *intellectual* order, and which can be no other than the mundane Gods. For the Demiurgus is chiefly characterized according to diversity, and is allotted the boundary of all universal hypostases.

All these orders are unfolded by Plato in the conclusions which the second hypothesis of his Parmenides contains; and this in a manner so perfectly agreeable to the Orphic and Chaldaic theology, that he who can read and *understand* the incomparable work of Proclus on Plato's theology will discover how ignorantly the latter Platonists have been abused by the moderns, as fanatics and corrupters of the doctrine of Plato.

According to the theology of Orpheus therefore, all things originate from an immense principle, to which through the imbecility and poverty of human conception we give a name, though it is perfectly ineffable, and in the reverential language of the Egyptians, is a *thrice unknown darkness*[16], in the contempla-

---

[16] " Of the first principle (says Damascius, in MS. περι αρχων) the Egyptians said nothing, but celebrated it as a darkness beyond all intellectual conception, a thrice unknown darkness," πρωτην αρχην ανυμνηκασων, σκοτος υπερ πασαν νοησιν, σκοτος αγνωστον, τρις τουτο επιφημιζοντες.

tion of which all knowledge is refunded into ignorance. Hence, as Plato says, in the conclusion of his first hypothesis in the Parmenides, " it can neither be named, nor spoken of, nor conceived by opinion, nor be known or perceived by any being." The peculiarity also of this theology, and in which its transcendency consists is this, that it does not consider the highest God to be simply the principle of beings, but *the principle of principles,* i. e. of deiform processions from itself, all which are eternally rooted in the unfathomable depths of the immensely great source of their existence, and of which they may be called superessential ramifications, and superluminous blossoms.

When the ineffable transcendency of the first God, which was considered (as I have elsewhere observed) to be the grand principle in the Heathen theology, by its most ancient promulgators, Orpheus, Pythagoras, and Plato, was forgotten, this oblivion was doubtless the cause of dead men being deified by the Pagans. Had they properly disposed their attention to this transcendency, they would have perceived it to be so immense as to surpass eternity, infinity, self-subsistence, and even essence itself, and that these in reality belong to those venerable natures which are as it were first unfolded into light from the arcane recesses of the truly mystic unknown cause of all. For, as Simplicius[17] beautifully observes, "It is requisite that he who ascends to the principle of things should investigate whether it is possible there can be any thing better than the supposed principle; and if something more excellent is found, the same inquiry should again be made respecting that, till we arrive at the highest conceptions, than which we have no longer any more venerable. Nor should we stop in our ascent till we find this to be the case. For there is no occasion to fear that our progression will be through an unsubstantial void, by conceiving something about the first principles which is greater than and surpasses their nature. *For it is not possible for our conceptions to take such a mighty leap as to equal, and much less to pass beyond the dignity of the first principles of things.*" He adds, "This therefore is one and the best extension [of the soul] to [the highest] God, and is as much as possible irreprehensible; viz. to know firmly, that by ascribing to him the most

---

[17] In Epictet.

venerable excellencies we can conceive, and the most holy and primary names and things, we ascribe nothing to him which is suitable to his dignity. It is sufficient, however, to procure our pardon [for the attempt] that we can attribute to him nothing superior." If it is not possible, therefore, to form any ideas equal to the dignity of the immediate progeny of the ineffable, i. e. of the first principles of things, how much less can our conceptions reach the principle of these principles, who is concealed in the superluminous darkness of occultly initiating silence? Had the Heathens therefore considered as they ought this transcendency of the supreme God and his immediate offspring, they never would have presumed to equalize the human with the divine nature, and consequently would never have worshiped men as Gods. Their theology, however, is not to be accused as the cause of this impiety, but their forgetfulness of the sublimest of its dogmas, and the confusion with which this oblivion was necessarily attended.

The following additional information also respecting the Orphic theology will greatly contribute to an elucidation of these Mystic Hymns: According to this theology, each of the Gods is in all, and all are in each, being ineffably united to each other and the highest God, because each being a superessential unity, their conjunction with each other is a union of unities. And hence it is by no means wonderful that each is celebrated as all. But another and a still more appropriate cause may be assigned of each of the celestial Gods being called by the appellations of so many other deities, which is this, that, according to the Orphic theology, each of the planets is fixed in a luminous etherial sphere called an ολοτης, or *wholeness*[18], because it is a part with a *total* subsistence, and is analogous to the sphere of the fixed stars. In consequence of this analogy, each of these planetary spheres contains a multitude of Gods, who are the satellites of the leading divinity of the sphere, and subsist conformably to his characteristics. This doctrine, which, as I have elsewhere observed, is one of the grand keys to the mythology and theology of the ancients, is not clearly delivered by any other ancient writer than Proclus, and has not, I believe, been noticed

---

[18] Each of these spheres is called a *wholeness*, because it contains a multitude of *partial* animals coordinate with it.

by any other modern author than myself. But the following are the passages in which this theory is unfolded by Proclus, in his admirable commentaries on the Timæus of Plato. "In each of the celestial spheres, the whole sphere has the relation of a monad, but the cosmocrators [or planets] are the leaders of the multitude in each. For in each a number analogous to the choir of the fixed stars subsists with appropriate circulations." (See vol. ii. book iv. p. 270, of my translation of this work.) And in another part of the same book (p. 280), "There are other divine animals following the circulations of the planets, the leaders of which are the seven planets; all which Plato comprehends in what is here said. For these also revolve and have a wandering of such a kind as that which he a little before mentioned of the seven planets. For they revolve in conjunction with and make their apocatastases together with their principals, just as the fixed stars are governed by the whole circulation [of the inerratic sphere]." And still more fully in p. 281, "Each of the planets is a whole world, comprehending in itself many divine genera invisible to us. Of all these, however, the visible star has the government.

And in this the fixed stars differ from those in the planetary spheres, that the former have one monad [viz. the inerratic sphere], which is the wholeness of them; but that in each of the latter there are invisible stars, which revolve together with their spheres; so that in each there is both the wholeness and a leader, which is alloted an exempt transcendency. For the planets, being secondary to the fixed stars, require a twofold prefecture, the one more total, but the other more partial. But that in each of these there is a multitude coordinate with each, you may infer from the extremes. For if the inerratic sphere has a multitude coordinate with itself, and earth is the wholeness of terrestrial, in the same manner as the inerratic sphere is of celestial animals, it is necessary that each intermediate wholeness should entirely possess certain partial animals coordinate with itself; through which, also, they are said to be wholenesses. The intermediate natures, however, are concealed from our sense, the extremes being manifest; one of them through its transcendently luminous essence, and the other through its alliance to us. If, likewise, partial souls [such as ours] are disseminated about them, some about the sun, others about the moon, and others about each of the rest, and prior to souls, dæmons give completion to the herds of which they are the leaders, it is evidently well said, that each of the spheres is a world; theologists also teaching us these things when they say that there are Gods in each prior to dæmons, some of which are under the government of others. Thus for instance, they assert concerning our mistress the Moon, that the Goddess Hecate is contained in her, and also Diana. Thus, too, in speaking of the sovereign Sun, and the Gods that are there, they celebrate Bacchus as being there,

> The Sun's assessor, who with watchful eye surveys
> The sacred pole.

They likewise celebrate the Jupiter who is there, Osiris, the solar Pan, and *others of which the books of theologists and theurgists are full*; from all which it is evident, that each of the planets is truly said to be the leader of many Gods, who give completion to its peculiar circulation."

From this extraordinary passage (as I have observed in a note on it in my Proclus, p. 282) we may perceive at one view why the

Sun in the Orphic Hymns is called Jupiter, why Apollo is called Pan, and Bacchus the Sun; why the Moon seems to be the same with Rhea, Ceres, Proserpine, Juno, Venus, &c. and, in short, why any one divinity is celebrated with the names and epithets of so many of the rest. For from this sublime theory it follows that every sphere contains a Jupiter, Neptune, Vulcan, Vesta, Minerva, Mars, Ceres, Juno, Diana, Mercury, Venus, Apollo, and in short every deity, each sphere at the same time conferring on these Gods the peculiar characteristic of its nature; so that, for instance, in the Sun they all possess a solar property, in the Moon a lunar one, and so of the rest. From this theory, too, we may perceive the truth of that divine saying of the ancients, that all things are full of Gods; for more particular orders proceed from such as are more general, the mundane from the supermundane, and the sublunary from the celestial; while earth becomes the general receptacle of the illuminations of all the Gods. "Hence," as Proclus shortly after observes, " there is a terrestrial Ceres, Vesta, and Isis, as likewise a terrestrial Jupiter and a terrestrial Hermes, established about the one divinity of the earth, just as a multitude of celestial Gods proceeds about the one divinity of the heavens. For there are progressions of all the celestial Gods into the Earth: and Earth contains all things, in an earthly manner, which Heaven comprehends celestially. Hence we speak of a terrestrial Bacchus and a terrestrial Apollo, who bestows the all-various streams of water with which the earth abounds, and openings prophetic of futurity." And if to all this we only add, that all the other mundane Gods subsist in the twelve abovementioned, and in short, all the mundane in the supermundane Gods, and that the first triad of these is *demiurgic* or *fabricative*, viz. Jupiter, Neptune, Vulcan; the second, Vesta, Minerva, Mars, *defensive*; the third, Ceres, Juno, Diana, *vivific*; and the fourth, Mercury, Venus, Apollo, *elevating* and *harmonic*; I say, if we unite this with the preceding theory, there is nothing in the ancient theology that will not appear admirably sublime and beautifully connected, accurate in all its parts, scientific and divine.

In the next place, that the following Hymns were written by Orpheus and that they were used in the Eleusinian Mysteries, will, I think,

xxxiv   INTRODUCTION.

be evident, from the following arguments, to the intelligent reader. For that hymns were written by Orpheus is testified by Plato in the eighth book of his Laws, and by Pausanias in his Boeotics, who also says that they were few and short; from whence, as Fabricius[19] justly observes, it appears that they were no other than those which are now extant[20]. But that they were used in the Eleusinian Mysteries is evident from the testimony of Lycomedes, who says that they were sung in the sacred rites pertaining to Ceres, which honour was not paid to the Homeric hymns, though they were more elegant than those of Orpheus; and the Eleusinian were the mysteries of Ceres. And that Lycomedes alludes, in what he here says, to these hymns is manifest, first from Pausanias, who in his Attics (cap. 37) observes, " that it is not lawful to ascribe the invention of beans to Ceres." He adds, " and he who has been initiated in the Eleusinian

---

[19] Vid. Biblioth. Græc. tom. i. p. 114.

[20] I omit the testimonies of Cyril contra Julian, lib. i. p. 25, and of Suidas, because their authority is of little value on this subject.

mysteries, *or has read the poems called Orphic*, will know what I mean." Now Porphyry De Abstinentia, lib. iv. informs us, that beans were forbidden in the Eleusinian mysteries[21]; and in the Orphic Hymn to *Earth* the sacrificer is ordered to fumigate from every kind of seed, except *beans* and aromatics. But Earth is Vesta, and Vesta, as we are informed by Proclus[22], is comprehended together with Juno in Ceres. Again, Suidas informs us, that τελετη signifies *a mystic sacrifice, the greatest and most venerable of all others*, (θυσια μυστηριωδης, η μεγιστη και τιμιωτατα). And Proclus, whenever he speaks of the Eleusinian mysteries, calls them the most holy *teletai*[23], αγιωταται τελεται. Agreeably to this, the Orphic Hymns are called in the Thryllitian manuscript τελεται; and Scaliger justly observes, that they contain nothing but such invocations as were used in the *mysteries*. Besides, many of the hymns are expressly thus called by the author of them. Thus the

---

[21] Παραγγελεται γαρ και Ελευσινι απεχεσθαι και κατοικιδων ορνιθων, και ιχθυων, και κυαμων, ροιας τε και μηλων. p. 353, Edit. Trajec.

[22] See the Additional Notes.

[23] In Plat. Theol. et in Comment. in Alcibiad.

conclusion of the hymn to Protogonus invokes that deity to be present at *the holy telete*, ες τελετην αγιαν: of the hymn to the Stars, to be present *at the very learned labours of the most holy telete;*

Ελθετ' επ' ευιερου τελετης πολυϊστορας αθλους.

And in the conclusion of the Hymn to Latona the sacrifice is called an *all-divine telete* (βαιν' επι πανθειον τελετην), as likewise in that of the Hymn to Amphietus Bacchus. And in short, the greater part of the hymns will be found to have either the word τελετη in them, or to invoke the respective divinities to bless *the mystics*, or *initiated persons*. Thus the conclusion of the Hymn to Heaven entreats that divinity to confer a blessed life on *a recent mystic:* the conclusion of the Hymn to the Sun, *to impart by illumination a pleasant life to the mystics:*

―――――― ηδυν δε βιον μυστρσι πρωφαινε.

And in a similar manner most of the other hymns [24].

[24] For a confirmation of this I refer the reader to the conclusions of the following hymns, viz. hymn vi, xviii,

Farther still, Demosthenes, in his first Oration against Aristogiton, has the following remarkable passage: και την απαραιτητον και σεμνην Δικην, ην ο τας αγιωτατας ημιν τελετας καταδειξας Ορφευς παρα τον του Διος θρονον φησι καθημενην, παντα τα των ανθρωπων εφοραν. i. e. "Let us reverence inexorable and venerable Justice, who is said by Orpheus, our instructor in the most holy *teletai*, to be seated by the throne of Jupiter, and to inspect all the actions of men." Here Demosthenes calls the mysteries *most holy*, as well as Proclus: and I think it may be concluded with the greatest confidence from all that has been said, that he alluded to the Hymn to Justice, which is one of the Orphic hymns, and to the following lines in that hymn:

Ομμα Δικης μελπω παλιδερκεος, αγλαομορφου,
Ἡ και Ζηνος ανακτος επι θρονον ιερον ιζει,
Ουρανοθεν καθορωσα βιον θνητων πολυφυλων.

---

xxiii, xxiv, xxv, xxxiv, xxxv, xlii, xliii, xliv, xlviii, l, lii, liii, liv, lvi, lvii, lviii, lx, lxi, lxxi, lxxiv, lxxvi, lxxvii, lxxviii, lxxix, lxxxiii, and lxxxv. And what is asserted in the eighty-fourth hymn, which is to Vesta, is particularly remarkable: for in the third line the poet says:

Τους δε συ εν τελεταις οσιους μυστας αναδειξαις.

i. e. You have appointed these holy *mystics in the teletæ*."

i. e. " I sing the all-seeing eye of splendid Justice, who sits by the throne of king Jupiter, and from her celestial abode beholds the life of multiform mortals."

The Eleusinian mysteries also, as is well known, were celebrated at night; the principal reason of which appears to be this, that the greater mysteries pertained to Ceres, and the less to Proserpine[25], and the latter preceded the former. But the rape of Proserpine, which was exhibited in these mysteries, signifies, as we are informed by Sallust[26], the descent of souls. And the descent of souls into the realms of generation is said, by Plato in the tenth book of his Republic, to take place at midnight, indicating by this the union of the soul with the darkness of a corporeal nature. This too, I suppose, is what Clemens Alexandrinus[27] means when

---

[25] Ησαν τα μεν μεγαλα της Δημητρος· τα δε μικρα Περσεφονης της αυτης θυγατρος. Interp. Græc. ad Plut. Aristophanis.

[26] De Diis et Mundo, cap. iv.

[27] Αι τελεται γινονται νυκτος μαλιστα, σημαινουσαι την εν νυκτι της ψυχης συστολην απο του σωματος. Clem. Alex. Stroma. lib. iv. p. 530, Sylburg.

he says, "that the mysteries were especially performed by night, thus signifying that the compression [i. e. confinement] of the soul by the body was effected at night." And that the sacrifices enjoined in the Orphic Hymns were performed by night, is evident from the hymn to Silenus, Satyrus, &c. in which Silenus, together with the Naiads, Bacchic Nymphs, and Satyrs, are implored to be present at the *nocturnal* orgies:

Οργια νυκτιφαη τελιταις αγιαις αναφαινων.

From all which I think it may be safely concluded, that these Hymns not only pertain to mysteries, but that they were used in the celebration of the Eleusinian, which by way of eminence (κατ' εξοχην) were called *the mysteries*, without any other note of distinction.

In the last place, it is requisite to speak of the author of these Hymns, and in addition to the evidence already adduced of their genuine antiquity, to vindicate them against those who contend that they are spurious, and were not written by Orpheus, but either by Onomacritus, or some poet who lived in the decline and fall of the Roman empire. And first, with respect to the dialect of these Hymns, Gesner observes, " that it ought to be no objection to their antiquity. For though according to Iamblichus[28], the Thracian Orpheus, who is more ancient than those noble poets Homer and Hesiod, used the Doric dialect; yet the Athenian Onomacritus, who according to the general opinion of antiquity is the author of all the works now extant ascribed to Orpheus, might either, preserving the sentences and a great part of the words, only change the dialect, and teach the ancient Orpheus to speak Homerically, or as I may say Solonically; or might arbitrarily add or take away what he thought proper, which, as we are informed by Herodotus, was his practice with respect to the Oracles." Gesner adds, " that it does not appear probable to him, that Onomacritus would dare to invent all that he wrote, since Orpheus must necessarily, at that time, have been much celebrated, and a great variety of his verses must have been in circulation." And he concludes with observing, " that the ob-

---

[28] De Vitâ Pythag. cap. xxxiv. p. 169. Kust.

INTRODUCTION. xli

jection of the Doric dialect ought to be of no more weight against the antiquity of the present works than the Pelasgic letters[19], which Orpheus, according to Diodorus Siculus, used.

In this extract, Gesner is certainly right in asserting that Onomacritus would not dare to invent all that he wrote, and afterwards publish it as Orphic; but I add, that it is unreasonable in the extreme to suppose that he in the least interpolated or altered the genuine works of Orpheus, though he might change the dialect in which they were originally written. For is it to be supposed that the Orphic Hymns would have been used in the Eleusinian mysteries, as we have demonstrated they were, if they had been spurious productions; or that the fraud would not have been long ago discovered by some of the many learned and wise men that flourished after Onomacritus; and that the detection of this fraud would not have been transmitted so as to reach even the present times? Or indeed, is it probable that such a forgery

---

[19] These letters are the old Etrurian or Eolian, and are perhaps more ancient than the Cadmian or Ionic.

could have existed at all, at a period when other learned men, as well as Onomacritus, had access to the genuine writings of Orpheus, and were equally capable with himself of changing them from one dialect into another? Even at a late period of antiquity, will any man who is at all familiar with the writings of Proclus, Hermias, and Olympiodorus, for a moment believe that men of such learning, profundity, and sagacity, would have transmitted to us so many verses as Orphic, though not in the Doric dialect, when at the same time they were the productions of Onamacritus? We may therefore, I think, confidently conclude, that though Onomacritus altered the dialect, he did not either add to or diminish, or in any respect adulterate the works of Orpheus; for it is impossible he should have committed such a fraud without being ultimately, if not immediately, detected.

With respect to those who contend that the works which are at present extant under the name of Orpheus were written during the decline and fall of the Roman empire, I trust every intelligent reader will deem it almost needless to say, in confutation of such an opinion, that it is an insult to the understanding of all the celebrated men of that period, by whom these writings have been quoted as genuine productions, and particularly to such among them as rank among the most learned, the most sagacious, and wisest of mankind. So infatuated, however, by this stupid opinion was Tyrwhitt, that in his edition of the Orphic poem Περι Λιθων (On Stones), he says in a note (p. 22) "there is nothing in the hymns peculiarly adapted to the person of Orpheus, except his speech to Musæus[30]." This speech or address to Musæus is the exordium to the Hymns. But so far is this from being true, that the author of this work expressly calls himself in two of the hymns *the son of Calliope.* Thus in the conclusion of the Hymn to the Nereids, the poet says,

Υμας γαρ πρωται τελετην ανεδειξατε σεμνην
Ευιερου Βακχοιο και αγνης Φερσεφονειης,
Καλλιοπη συν μητρι, και Απολλωνι ανακτι.

i. e. " For you at first disclos'd the rites divine,
    Of holy Bacchus, and of Proserpine,

---

[30] " In Hymnis nihil est ad personam Orphei peculiariter accommodatum, nisi allocutio ad Musæum."

Of fair Calliope, from whom I spring,
And of Apollo bright, the Muses' king."

And in the Hymn to the Muses, he celebrates Calliope as his mother, in the very same words as in the Hymn to the Nerieds, Καλλιοπη συν μητρι. This blunder of Tyrwhitt is certainly a most egregious specimen of the folly of pervicacious adherence to an opinion which had ignorance and prejudice only for its source, and which calumniated writings far beyond the *little sphere* of its knowledge to comprehend.

As to Orpheus himself, the original author of these Hymns, scarcely a vestige of his life is to be found amongst the immense ruins of time. For who has ever been able to affirm any thing with certainty of his origin, his age, his country, and condition. This alone may be depended on, from general assent, that there formerly lived a person named Orpheus, who was the founder of theology among the Greeks; the institutor of their life and morals; the first of prophets, and the prince of poets; himself the offspring of a Muse; who taught the Greeks their sacred rites and mysteries, and from whose wisdom, as from a perennial and abundant fountain, the divine muse of Homer and the sublime theology of Pythagoras and Plato flowed.

The following, however, is a summary of what has been transmitted to us by the ancients concerning the original Orpheus, and the great men who have at different periods flourished under this venerable name. The first and genuine Orpheus is said to have been a Thracian, and according to the opinion of many was a disciple of Linus[31], who flourished at the time when the kingdom of the Athenians was dissolved. Some assert that he was prior to the Trojan war, and that he lived eleven, or as others say nine, generations. But the Greek word γενεα, or *generation*, signifies, according to Gyraldus[32], the space of seven years: for unless this is admitted, how is it possible that the period of his life can have any foundation in the nature of things? If this signification therefore of the word is adopted, Orpheus lived either seventy-seven or sixty-three years, the latter of which, if we may believe astrologers, is a fatal period, and especially to

---

[31] Vid. Suid. [32] Syntag. Poet. p. 54.

great men, as it proved to be to Aristotle and Cicero.

Our poet, according to fabulous tradition, was torn in pieces by Ciconian women; on which account Plutarch affirms the Thracians were accustomed to beat their wives, in order that they might revenge the death of Orpheus. Hence in the vision of Herus Pamphilius, in the tenth book of Plato's Republic, the soul of Orpheus, being destined to descend into another body, is said to have chosen that of a swan, rather than to be born again of a woman; having conceived such a hatred of the sex, on account of his violent death. The cause of his destruction is variously related by authors. Some report that it arose from his being engaged in puerile loves, after the death of Eurydice. Others, that he was destroyed by women intoxicated with wine, because he was the cause of men relinquishing an association with them. Others again assert, according to Pausanias, that on the death of Eurydice, wandering to Aornus, a place in Thesprotia, where it was customary to evocate the souls of the dead, having recalled Eurydice to life, and not being able to detain her, he destroyed himself; nightingales bringing forth their young on his tomb, whose melody exceeded every other of this species. Others again, ascribe his laceration to his having celebrated every divinity except Bacchus, which is very improbable, as among the following hymns there are nine to that deity, under different appellations. Others report that he was delivered by Venus herself into the hands of the Ciconian women, because his mother Calliope had not determined justly between Venus and Proserpine concerning the young Adonis. Many affirm, according to Pausanias, that he was struck by lightning; and Diogenes confirms this by the following verses, composed, as he asserts, by the Muses on his death:

> Here by the Muses plac'd, with golden lyre,
> Great Orpheus rests, destroy'd by heavenly fire.

Again, the sacred mysteries called Threscian derived their appellation from the Thracian bard, because he first introduced sacred rites and religion into Greece; and hence the authors of initiation into these mysteries were called Orpheotelestæ. Besides, according to Lucian, Orpheus brought astrology and the magical arts into Greece; and as to his drawing to him trees and wild beasts by the melody of his lyre, Palæphatus[33] accounts for it as follows: " The mad Bacchanalian Nymphs, says he, having violently taken away cattle and other necessaries of life, retired for some days into the mountains. But the citizens, having expected their return for a long time, and fearing the worst for their wives and daughters, called Orpheus, and entreated him to invent some method of drawing them from the mountains. Orpheus, in consequence of this, tuning his lyre conformably to the orgies of Bacchus, drew the mad nymphs from their retreats; who descended from the mountains, bearing at first ferulæ, and branches of every kind of trees. But to the men who were eyewitnesses of these wonders, they appeared to bring down the very woods, and from hence gave rise to the fable[34].

---

[33] Vid. Opusc. Mythol. p. 45.

[34] The true meaning of the fable however, in my opinion, is this, that Orpheus by his sacred doctrines tamed men of *rustic* and *savage* dispositions. But the most careless

So great indeed was the renown of Orpheus, that he was deified by the Greeks; and Philostratus relates, that his head gave oracles in Lesbos, which when separated from his body by the Thracian women, was, together with his lyre, carried down the river Hebrus into the sea. In this manner, says Lucian, singing as it were his funeral oration, to which the chords of his lyre, impelled by the winds, gave a responsive harmony, it was brought to Lesbos and buried. But his lyre was suspended in the temple of Apollo; where it remained for a considerable space of time. Afterwards, when Neanthus, the son of Pittacus the tyrant, found that the lyre drew trees and wild beasts by its harmony, he earnestly desired to possess it;

---

readers must be struck with the similitude of the latter part of this fable to what took place at the wood of Birnam in Shakspeare's Macbeth; and to which the following lines allude:

"Macbeth shall never vanquished be, until
Great Birnam wood to high Dunsinane hill
Shall come against him."

This coincidence, however, has not been noticed by any of the commentators of Shakspeare.

and having corrupted the priest privately with money, he took the Orphic lyre, and fixed another similar to it in the temple. But Neanthus considering, that he was not safe in the city in the day, departed from it by night; having concealed the lyre in his bosom, on which he began to play. As however he was a rude and unlearned youth, he confounded the chords; yet pleasing himself with the sound, and fancying he produced a divine harmony, he thought himself to be the blessed successor of Orpheus. But in the midst of his transports, the neighbouring dogs, roused by the sound, fell on the unhappy harper and tore him in pieces.

The former part of this fable is thus admirably explained by Proclus, in his Commentaries (or rather fragments of Commentaries) on the Republic of Plato, " Orpheus (says he), on account of his perfect erudition, is reported to have been destroyed in various ways; because, as it appears to me, men of that age participated *partially* of the Orphic harmony: for they were incapable of receiving a universal and perfect science. But the principal part of his melody [i. e. of his mystic doctrine] was received by the Lesbians; and on this account, perhaps, the head of Orpheus, when separated from his body, is said to have been carried to Lesbos. Fables of this kind, therefore, are related of Orpheus no otherwise than of Bacchus, of whose mysteries he was the priest."

The second Orpheus was an Arcadian, or, according to others, a Ciconian, from the Thracian Bisaltia, and is said to be more ancient than Homer and the Trojan war. He composed fabulous figments called (μυθοποιιαι) and epigrams. The third Orpheus was of Odrysius, a city of Thrace, near the river Hebrus; but Dionysius in Suidas denies his existence. The fourth Orpheus was of Crotonia; flourished in the time of Pisistratus, about the fiftieth Olympiad, and is, I have no doubt, the same with Onamacritus, who changed the dialect of these hymns. He wrote Decennalia (δεκαετηρια), and in the opinion of Gyraldus the Argonautics, which are now extant under the name of Orpheus, with other writings called Orphical, but which according to Cicero[35] some ascribe to Cecrops the Pythagorean. But the last Or-

---

[35] In lib. i. de Nat. Decr.

pheus was Camarinæus, a most excellent versifier; and the same, according to Gyraldus, whose descent into Hades is so universally known.

I shall only add to this historical detail respecting Orpheus, what Hermias excellently remarks in his Scholia on the Phædrus of Plato. "You may see, says he, how Orpheus appears to have applied himself to all these [i. e. to the four kinds of mania[36]], as being in want of, and adhering to, each other. For we learn that he was most *telestic*, and most *prophetic*, and was excited by Apollo; and besides this, that he was most *poetic*, on which account he is said to have been the son of Calliope. He was likewise most *amatory*, as he himself acknowledges to Musæus, extending to him divine benefits, and rendering him perfect. Hence he appears to have been possessed by all the manias, and this by a necessary consequence. For there is an abundant union, conspiration, and alliance with each other of the Gods who preside over these manias, viz. of the Muses, Bacchus, Apollo, and Love."

[36] i. e. The *telestic*, or pertaining to the mysteries, the *prophetic*, the *poetic*, and the *amatory*.

INTRODUCTION.

With respect to the following translation, it is requisite to observe, that I have adopted rhyme, not because most agreeable to the general taste, but because I conceive it to be necessary to the poetry of the English language; which requires something as a substitute for the energetic cadence of the Greek and Latin hexameters. Could this be obtained by any other means, I should immediately relinquish my partiality for rhyme, which is certainly, when well executed, far more difficult than blank verse, as these Orphic Hymns must evince in an eminent degree.

Indeed, where languages differ so much as the ancient and modern, the most perfect method perhaps of transferring the poetry of the former tongue into that of the latter is by a faithful and animated paraphrase; faithful, with regard to retaining the meaning of the author; and animated, with respect to preserving the fire of the original; calling it forth when latent, and expanding it when condensed. He who is anxious to effect this will every where endeavour to diffuse the light and fathom the depth of his author; to elucidate what is obscure, and to amplify what in modern language would be unintelligibly concise.

Thus, most of the compound epithets of which the following hymns chiefly consist, though extremely beautiful in the Greek language, yet when literally translated into ours lose much of their propriety and force. In their native tongue, as in a prolific soil, they diffuse their sweets with full blown elegance; and he who would preserve their theological beauties, and exhibit them to others in a different language, must expand their elegance by the supervening and enlivening rays of a light derived from mystic lore; and, by the powerful breath of genius, scatter abroad their latent but copious sweets.

If it shall appear that the translator has possessed some portion of this light, and has diffused it in the following work, he will consider himself to be well rewarded for his laborious undertaking. The philosophy of Plato, and the theology of the Greeks, have been for the greater part of his life the only study of his retired leisure; in which he has found an inexhaustible treasure of intellectual wealth, and a perpetual fountain of wisdom and delight. Presuming, therefore, that such a pursuit must be a great advantage to the present undertaking, and feeling the most sovereign contempt for the sordid drudgery of venal composition, he desires no other reward, if he has succeeded, than the praise of the liberal; and no other defence, if he has failed, than the decision of the candid and discerning few.

THE
MYSTICAL HYMNS
OF
ORPHEUS.

THE

Mystical Hymns of Orpheus.

TO MUSÆUS[1].

LEARN, O Musæus, from my sacred song
What rites most fit to sacrifice[2] belong.
Jove I invoke, the earth, and solar light,
The moon's pure splendour, and the stars of night.

[1] The Greek Scholiast on Aristophanes (in Ranis) observes, that Musæus was the offspring of the Moon and Eumolpus; that according to Sophocles he uttered oracles; and that he composed παραλυσεις, τελεται and καθαρμοι. Of these works, which are unfortunately lost, the παραλυσεις or καταλυσεις, taught both individuals and cities how by religious ceremonies they might be liberated from the punishment attendant on the crimes which they had committed. His τελεται, or Mysteries, are mentioned by Plato, Lucian, and others. And the καθαρμοι contained the means of expiating and becoming *purified* from guilt.

[2] For a copious developement of sacrifices, and of the utility or power they possess in the universe, and also on what account they were anciently performed, see Book the Second of my translation of Porphyry's excellent Treatise on Abstinence from Animal Food; and Sect. V. of my translation of Iamblichus on the Mysteries. Likewise, for an account of Theurgy, or the art pertaining to divine operations, see the latter of the abovementioned works, and the accompanying notes.

Thee, Neptune, ruler of the sea profound,
Dark-hair'd, whose power can shake the solid ground;
Ceres abundant, and of lovely mien,
And thee, chaste Proserpine, great Pluto's queen;
The huntress Dian, and bright Phœbus' rays,
Far darting God, the theme of Delphic praise;
And Bacchus, honour'd by the heav'nly choir,
Impetuous Mars, and Vulcan, God of fire.
Th' illustrious power who sprung from foam to light,
And Pluto, potent in the realms of night;
With Hebe young, and Hercules the strong,
And you to whom the cares of births belong.
Justice and Piety august I call,
And much fam'd Nymphs, and Pan the God of all.
To Juno sacred, and to Mem'ry fair,
And the chaste Muses I address my pray'r;
The various Year, the Graces, and the Hours,
Fair-hair'd Latona, and Dione's pow'rs.
The Corybantes and Curetes armed I call[3],
And the great Saviours, sons of Jove, the king of all:
Th' Idæan Gods, the angel of the skies,
Prophetic Themis with sagacious eyes,
With ancient Night, and Daylight I implore,
And Faith and Dice source of blameless laws adore;

---

[3] In the translation of many of these hymns, I have been obliged to employ an Alexandrine line, as well as in this and the following line, in order to preserve the meaning of the author.

Saturn and Rhea, and great Thetis too,
Hid in a veil of dark celestial blue.
I call great Ocean, and the beauteous train
Of Ocean's daughters in the boundless main:
The strength of Atlas ever in its prime,
Vig'rous Eternity, and endless Time.
The splendid Stygian pool, and placid Gods beside,
And dæmons good and bad that o'er mankind preside;
Illustrious Providence, the noble train
Of dæmon forms, who fill th' etherial plain;
Or live in air, in water, earth, or fire,
Or deep beneath the solid ground retire.
The white Leucothea of the sea I call,
And Semele, and Bacchus's associates all;
Palæmon bounteous, and Adrastia[4] great,
And sweet-tongu'd Victory, with success elate;

[4] This divinity is one among others in this Exordium to whom there is no hymn in these Orphic Teletæ. But the following particulars respecting this Goddess, extracted from the Scholia of Hermeas on the Phædrus of Plato, are given on account of their great importance, and because they illustrate a part of the Orphic theology. "Adrastia is a divinity seated in the vestibules of Night, and is the offspring of Melissus and Amalthea. Melissus, therefore, is to be assumed as a power providentially attending to secondary natures; but Amalthea must be considered according to the unchanging and the uneffeminate. Hence Adrastia was generated from unchangeable Providence, and she is the sister of Ida.

> The beauteous Ida and Adrastia sprung
> From the same sire.

Great Esculapius, skill'd to cure disease,
And dread Minerva, whom fierce battles please;
Thunders, and Winds in mighty columns pent,
With dreadful roaring struggling hard for vent;
Attis, the mother of the pow'rs on high,
Mensis, and pure Adonis, never doom'd to die,

This Goddess, therefore, comprehends in transcendent union, and contains in herself at once the centres of all laws, viz. of the mundane and the supermundane, of those of Fate, and those of Jupiter: for there are Jovian and Saturnian, divine, supermundane, and mundane laws. On this account she is called Adrastia, because her legislative decrees are inevitable. Hence she is said to be seated with brazen drumsticks in her hands, before the cave of Night, and through the sound produced by her cymbals to render all things obedient to her laws. For Phanes indeed is seated within the cave, in the Adytum of Night; but Night sits in the middle of the cave, prophesying to the Gods; and Adrastia sits in the vestibules, legislatively promulgating the divine laws. She differs, however, from the justice which is there, after the same manner as the legislative differs from the judicial characteristic. And the justice which is there is said to be the daughter of the Law and Piety which are there. But Adrastia herself, who is the offspring of Melissus and Amalthea, is likewise comprehensive of Law. These, therefore, are said to have nurtured Jupiter in the cavern of Night; the theologist [Orpheus] directly asserting that which Plato says about Jupiter. For Plato represents him fabricating and promulgating laws. But divine law is imparted by Adrastia to the Gods also: for the order which is in them is derived from this Goddess. It is, however, likewise imparted to the attendants of the Gods, and in common to all, and peculiarly to each."

End and Beginning (greatest this to all),
These with propitious aid I suppliant call,
To this libation, and these sacred rites;
For these t' accede with joyful mind, my verse invites.

I.

TO HECATE.

EINODIAN Hecate[5], Trivia, lovely dame,
Of earthly, wat'ry, and celestial frame,
Sepulchral, in a saffron veil array'd,
Pleas'd with dark ghosts that wander thro' the shade;
Persæa[6], solitary goddess, hail!
The world's key-bearer, never doom'd to fail;
In stags rejoicing, huntress, nightly seen,
And drawn by bulls, unconquerable queen;

---

[5] Io. Diac. Allegor. ad Hesiodi Theog. p. 268, cites this line, on which, and Hymn 71. 3, he observes: Ευρισκω, τον Ορφεα και την Τυχην Αρτεμιν προσαγορευοντα, αλλα και την Σεληνην Εκατην. i. e. "I find that Orpheus calls Fortune Artemis or Diana, and also the Moon Hecate."

[6] Diodorus informs us, that Diana, who is to be understood by this epithet, was very much worshiped by the Persians, and that this Goddess was called *Persæa* in his time. See more concerning this epithet in Gyrald. Syntag. ii. p. 361.

Leader, nymph, nurse, on mountains wand'ring, hear
The suppliants who with holy rites thy power revere,
And to the *herdsman*[7] with a fav'ring mind draw near[8].

II.

TO THE GODDESS PROTHYRÆA[9].

THE FUMIGATION FROM STORAX.

O VENERABLE Goddess, hear my pray'r,
For labour pains are thy peculiar care.
In thee, when stretch'd upon the bed of grief,
The sex, as in a mirror, view relief.

[7] As Orpheus by his sacred doctrines tamed men of a *rustic and savage* disposition; which, as we have before observed, appears to be the true meaning of the fable of his drawing to him *trees and wild beasts* by the melody of his lyre; hence, alluding to this circumstance, he calls himself here, and in the hymn to the Curetes, *the herdsman*, indicating the benefit which he conferred on the vulgar part or *herd* of mankind.

[8] In all the editions of these hymns, prior to that of Hermann, this hymn forms a part of the exordium to Musæus; but it is certainly better to separate it from that exordium, though I did not perceive the propriety of doing so in the former edition of this translation.

[9] This is an epithet of Diana, alluding to her presiding over gates, and being as it were the gate-keeper of life. In a hymn which was first discovered by me among the Har-

Guard of the race, endued with gentle mind,
To helpless youth benevolent and kind;
Benignant nourisher; great Nature's key
Belongs to no divinity but thee.
Thou dwell'st with all immanifest to sight,
And solemn festivals are thy delight.
Thine is the task to loose the virgin's zone,
And thou in ev'ry work art seen and known.
With births you sympathize, tho' pleas'd to see
The numerous offspring of fertility.
When rack'd with labour pangs, and sore distress'd,
The sex invoke thee, as the soul's sure rest;
For thou alone canst give relief to pain,
Which art attempts to ease, but tries in vain.
Assisting Goddess, venerable pow'r,
Who bring'st relief in labour's dreadful hour;
Hear, blessed Dian, and accept my pray'r,
And make the infant race thy constant care.

leian MSS. in the British Museum, and which, from the manner of it, was, I have no doubt, written by Proclus, *Hecate* is called *Prothyræa*. For the second line of this hymn, which is entitled Υμνος Κοινος, or a *Common Hymn*, is

Χαιρ' Εκατη, Προθυραιε, μεγασθενες, αλλος εαυτος.

See the whole of this hymn in the original, and also a translation of it at the end of my *Collectanea*.

III.

TO NIGHT.

THE FUMIGATION WITH TORCHES.

NIGHT, parent Goddess, source of sweet repose,
From whom at first both Gods and men arose [10].

[10] The first subsistence of the Goddess Night is at the summit of that divine order which is denominated by Chaldean theologists νοητος και νοερος, i. e. *intelligible and at the same time intellectual.* This order is denominated by Plato, in the Phædrus, the supercelestial place, and in which he says *the plain of Truth* is situated, which, as we are informed by Hermeas (in Phædr.) obscurely indicates the whole order of the series of Night. What Hermeas afterwards adds on this subject is too important to be omitted, and is as follows:—" Theologists likewise peculiarly establish *Truth* in the supercelestial place." For Orpheus, speaking about Night, says, that " she possesses the truth* of the Gods," and

To her, prediction wholly *true* was giv'n.

She is also said to prophesy to the Gods. Homer, too, indicates concerning this Goddess. For, speaking about Jupiter, Sleep says,

Night, the great tamer both of Gods and men,
To whom I fled, preserv'd me from his wrath;
For he swift† Night was fearful to offend.

* In the original αληθειαν is omitted in this place, but evidently ought to be inserted.

† As Night, from her subsistence at the summit of the intelligible and at the same time intellectual order, is absorbed in the intelligible, hence Homer divinely denominates Night *swift*. For the Chaldean Oracles call the intelligible Gods *swift*.

Hear, blessed Venus[11], deck'd with starry light,
In Sleep's deep silence dwelling Ebon night!

But Plato says he shall *dare* to speak concerning it, because he is going to assert something *affirmatively* about it. The *dread*, however, is lest we should be led to something unappropriate and vile in such like doctrinal concerns. He is also concordant in what he says about the supercelestial place, with what he asserts in [the first hypothesis of] the Parmenides, about the first principle of things. For he there indicates this principle by negations; except that he absolutely denies all things of the first principle: but of the supercelestial place he denies some things, and affirms others. For the Goddess Night is superior to certain orders, but inferior to others; and as the first principle of things is superessential, so Night is supercelestial [i. e. is above that intellectual order which is denominated Heaven]. Why, however, are souls not said to see Heaven, but to become situated in, and be conjoined with it, yet are not conjoined with the natures above Heaven, but perceive them only? In answer to this it may be said, that it is necessary contact should exist, as far as to a certain thing. Why, therefore, as far as to this? Because neither are the Gods under Jupiter said to be united to Phanes; but this is alone asserted of Jupiter, and he is said to be united through *Night* as a medium.

But how does Plato say, that the supercelestial place is without colour? Is it in the same manner as we say, that

---

[11] Hermann is of opinion that the line Νυξ γενεσις παντων, ην και Κυπριν καλεσωμεν, i. e. "Night, the source of all things, whom we also call Venus," is an interpolation. But there is no reason whatever for this supposition: for Venus in the hymn to her is called νυκτερια, and φιλοπαννυχε σεμνη.

Dreams and soft ease attend thy dusky train,
Pleas'd with the length'ned gloom and feastful strain,

nature and soul are colourless? But what is there admirable
in asserting this? And if we admit this, what* will there
be transcendent in the supercelestial place, since the same
thing is possessed both by nature and soul? May we not
say that Plato, in what is here asserted, very much follows the beforementioned theologists [viz. Homer, Orpheus,
Hesiod, and Musæus], and disposes what he says conformably to them? For after the order of *Nights* there are
three orders of Gods, viz. of Heaven, the Cyclops, and the
Centimani [or Gods with a hundred hands], the proper
names of whom Plato denies of the supercelestial place.
For of the Gods which abide within Phanes, Heaven is
the first that becomes visible from him; for Heaven and
Earth first proceeded out of Phanes; and Heaven is first
illuminated by the divine light of Phanes; since Orpheus
says that Night is united to him:

> No eye but that of sacred Night alone
> Beheld Protogonus; for all the rest
> Were lost in wonder at th' unhop'd for light,
> Which glitter'd from th' immortal Phanes' skin.

But that which is visible and illuminated is coloured, since
colours are certain illuminations. Hence Night and all the
supercelestial place, being above Heaven, which is visible,
they are very properly said to be without colour. For
night also is opposed to day, because the latter is illuminated and coloured. And through *the privation of colour*,
indeed, Plato manifests that the place of the Nights is above
the kingdom of the Heaven; but through *the privation of
figure*, that it is above the order of the Cyclops. For theology says, that figure is first unfolded into light in these,

---

* For τοι here, it is necessary to read η, and to make the sentence in-
terrogatory.

Dissolving anxious care, the friend of mirth,
With darkling coursers riding round the earth.

and that the divinities, the Cyclops, are the first principles
and causes of the figures which subsist every where. Hence
theology says, that they are *manual artificers*. For this
triad * is perfective of figures.

And in their forehead one round eye was fix'd†.

In the Parmenides, likewise, Plato, when he speaks of the
straight, the circular, and that which is mixed‡ [from both
these], obscurely indicates this order. But these Cyclops,
as being the first causes of figures, taught Minerva and
Vulcan the various species of figures.

These the first manual artists were, who taught
Pallas and Vulcan all things:

[says Orpheus]. We must not therefore wonder on hearing
that Vulcan and Minerva are the causes of figures. For
Vulcan is the cause of corporeal figures, and of every mundane figure; but Minerva, of the psychical and intellectual
figure; and the Cyclops of divine, and the every where
existing figure. Hence it is evident, that the supercelestial
place is above the order of the Cyclops.

But by *the privation of contact* Plato manifests that this
place is above the *Centimani;* for these first come into contact, as it were, with all the fabrication of things. Hence
theology denominates them *hundred-handed:* for through the
hands we touch, make, and distinguish all things. Farther
still, the touch pervades through the whole body. Theology

---

* The triad of the Cyclops consists of Brontes, Steropes, and Arges.

† Hesiod Theog. 145.

‡ The words και το μικτον are omitted in the original, but ought to be inserted, as will be evident from a perusal of the first hypothesis of the Parmenides.

Goddess of phantoms and of shadowy play,
Whose drowsy pow'r divides the nat'ral day;

therefore, symbolically, calls these *hundred-handed*, as *touching* all the fabrication of things, and being the causes of it. The triad*, however, of the Centimani is of a guardian nature. But Plato adduces negatively what he found celebrated affirmatively by the theologist. For what Orpheus calls *Night*, that Plato denominates *without colour*. And what the former says negatively is *without falsehood*,

> Prediction without falsehood was to Night
> Of all things giv'n. [says Orpheus.]

that the latter celebrates, as *having about it the genus of true science*, and *as being truly existing essence*. Plato also, having celebrated the supercelestial place by three negations, again adduces three affirmations, introducing three of them from being. For, since this order is a triadic one, Plato very properly preserves the triadic, both in the negative and affirmative conclusions. Or it may be said that, since it is both one and being, and is triadic according to each of these, he indicates the negative conclusions according to the superessential one, but the affirmative according to being. Here likewise the first number is unfolded into light."

In the next place Hermeas enumerates the different kinds of Truth, as follows: " Superior illuminate subordinate natures with the light of Truth. We must extend the eye of intellect therefore to these four; viz. *the one*, which is the first principle of things; Phanes, who is the boundary of the intelligible, but the exempt principle of the intellectual Gods (for the Nights are principles with which principle is co-ordinate); Jupiter, who is the king of the supermundane, but the boundary of what are properly called the

---

* This triad consists of Cottus, Gyges, and Briareus.

By Fate's decree you constant send the light
To deepest hell, remote from mortal sight;
For dire Necessity, which nought withstands,
Invests the world with adamantine bands.
Be present, Goddess, to thy suppliant's pray'r,
Desir'd by all, whom all alike revere,
Blessed, benevolent, with friendly aid
Dispel the fears of twilight's dreadful shade.

intellectual Gods; and the Sun, who is the king of sensible natures. But each of these illuminates the beings that are under* it with the truth, which it possesses from an order placed above that which it illuminates. Thus the Sun imparts supermundane light to sensibles; and hence the essence of it is said to be from supermundane natures. Again, Jupiter illuminates supermundane essences with intellectual light. Phanes illuminates the intellectual Gods with intelligible light; and the principle of all things fills the intelligible Gods, and all things, with the divine light proceeding from himself†.

* For υπαι here, it is obviously necessary to read υπο.
† Instead of απ' αυτων in this place, it is requisite to read απ' αυτου.

IV.

TO HEAVEN.

THE FUMIGATION FROM FRANKINCENSE.

Great Heav'n, whose mighty frame no respite knows,
Father of all, from whom the world arose;
Hear, bounteous parent, source and end of all,
For ever whirling round this earthly ball;
Abode of Gods, whose guardian pow'r surrounds
Th' eternal world with ever during bounds [12];
Whose ample bosom, and encircling folds
The dire necessity of nature holds.
Etherial, earthly [13], whose all-various frame,
Azure and full of forms, no power can tame.
All-seeing, source of Saturn and of time,
For ever blessed, deity sublime,
Propitious on a novel mystic shine,
And crown his wishes with a life divine.

---

[12] According to Orpheus, as we are informed by Damascius περι αρχων, "Heaven is the boundary and guardian of all things," ο του Ορφεος Ουρανος ουρος και παντων φυλαξ ειναι βουλεται.

[13] The dogma that subordinate natures are causally contained in such as are supreme, and such as are supreme in

V.

TO ETHER.

THE FUMIGATION FROM SAFFRON.

O EVER untam'd Ether, rais'd on high
In Jove's dominions, ruler of the sky;
Great portion of the Stars and lunar light,
And of the Sun, with dazzling lustre bright;
All-taming pow'r, ethereal shining fire,
Whose vivid blasts the heat of life inspire;
The world's best element, light-bearing pow'r,
With starry radiance shining, splendid flow'r;
O hear my suppliant pray'r, and may thy frame
Be ever innocent, serene, and tame.

---

the subordinate by participation, is originally Egyptian, but is also said by Proclus, in Tim. p. 292, to be Orphical. For in enumerating the Orphic traditions concerning Phanes, Night, Heaven, Saturn, Jupiter, and Bacchus, he observes, εστι γαρ και εν Γη Ουρανος, και εν Ουρανῳ Γῃ (lege Γη)· και ἐνταυθα μεν ο Ουρανος χθονιως, εκει δὲ ουρανιως η Γη· και γαρ ουρανιαν και την (lege γην την) Σεληνην Ορφευς προσηγορευσεν. i. e. " For Heaven is in Earth, and Earth in Heaven. And here indeed [i. e. in the Earth] Heaven subsists terrestrially; but there [in the heavens] Earth subsists celestially. For Orpheus also calls the Moon *celestial earth.*"

VI.

TO PROTOGONUS[14].

THE FUMIGATION FROM MYRRH.

O MIGHTY first-begotten, hear my pray'r,
Twofold, egg-born, and wand'ring thro' the air;
Bull-roarer[15], glorying in thy golden wings,
From whom the race of Gods and mortal springs.

---

[14] According to Orpheus, as related by Syrianus, in Metaph. Arist. p. 114, the first principle of all things is *the one*, or *the good itself*; and after this, conformably to the doctrine of Pythagoras, the two principles, *ether* and *chaos*, subsist. And of these principles, the first, or *ether*, is analogous to *bound*; and the second, or *chaos*, to *infinity*. Afterwards, says Syrianus, the first and occult genera of the Gods subsist, among which the first apparent God is the king and father of the universe, who, because he is the first visible deity, is denominated Phanes. The whole of this first and occult genera of the Gods, which is called by the Chaldean theologists the intelligible triad, was represented by Orpheus under the symbol of an egg, on the exclusion of which by the Goddess Night, the God Phanes came forth, who is hence denominated Protogonus.

[15] Phanes, or Protogonus, who subsists at the extremity of the intelligible triad, and is therefore νους νοητος, or *intelligible intellect*, and the exemplar of the universe, is denominated by Plato in the Timæus το αυτοζωον, *animal itself*, as being the primordial cause of all animal life, and was symbolically represented by Orpheus as adorned with the heads of a ram, a *bull*, a serpent, and a lion. But Jupiter,

Ericapæus, celebrated pow'r,
Ineffable, occult, all-shining flow'r.
'Tis thine from darksome mists to purge the sight[16],
All-spreading splendour, pure and holy light;

or the demiurgus of the universe, is in the intellectual what Phanes is in the intelligible order of Gods; and hence he is said by Orpheus to have absorbed Phanes prior to his fabrication of the world; the theologist indicating by this his participation of all the primary paradigmatic causes of things which subsist in Phanes. As Porphyry, therefore, in his treatise De Antro Nympharum, informs us,' " that the Persian deity Mithra, as well as the *bull*, is the demiurgus and lord of generation, the reason is obvious why Protogonus is called in this hymn *bull-roarer*, the roaring signifying the procession of ideas to the formation of the world. And this is conformable to what is asserted respecting ideas in the Chaldæan oracle , viz.

Νους πατρος ερροιζησε νοησας ακμαδι βουλη
Παμμορφους ιδεας.

i. e. " The intellect of the father made a crashing noise, understanding with unwearied counsel omniform ideas." For the *crashing noise* indicates the same thing as the *roaring* of Protogonus.

[16] This line in the original is,

Οσσων ος σκοτοεσσαν απημαυρωσας ομιχλην.

And Proclus, in the Fifth Book of his MS. Commentary on the Parmenides of Plato, evidently, as it appears to me, alludes to this verse. For, speaking of the intelligible monad, or the summit of the intelligible order, at the extremity of which Protogonus subsists, he says, " It is by no means wonderful if this monad comprehends the whole intellectual pentad, viz. essence, motion, permanency, same-

Hence, Phanes, call'd the glory of the sky,
On waving pinions thro' the world you fly.
Priapus, dark-ey'd splendour[17], thee I sing,
Genial, all-prudent, ever blessed king.
With joyful aspect on these rites divine
And holy Telite propitious shine.

ness, and difference, without division, and in the most profound union; since through this union all these are after a manner one. For all things are there without separation, according to a *dark mist*, as the theologist asserts." Αδιακριτων παντων οντων κατα σκοτοεσσαν ομιχλην. In which passage the two last words form a part of the above Orphic line.

But the reason why Protogonus, or Phanes, is said *to purge the sight from dark mists*, is because the primary causes of things which in the deities prior to him subsist in ineffable union, all being in all, are by him first unfolded into intelligible light.

[17] Protogonus, who is *intelligible intellect*, is very properly called *dark-eyed splendour;* the intelligible, from its occult subsistence, being indicated by *darkness*, but intellect by the *eye* and *splendour:* for it is the province of intellect to *see and unfold into light.*

VII.

TO THE STARS.

THE FUMIGATION FROM AROMATICS.

With holy voice I call the stars on high,
Pure sacred lights, and dæmons of the sky.
Celestial stars, dear progeny of Night,
In whirling circles beaming far your light;
Refulgent rays around the heav'ns ye throw,
Eternal fires, the source of all below.
With flames significant of Fate ye shine,
And aptly rule for men a path divine.
In seven bright zones ye run with wand'ring flames,
And heaven and earth[18] compose your lucid frames:
With course unwearied, pure and fiery bright,
For ever shining thro' the veil of Night.
Hail, glittering, joyful, ever wakeful fires!
Propitious shine on all my just desires,
These sacred rites regard with conscious rays,
And end our works devoted to your praise.

[18] As Heaven, in the hymn to that divinity, is said to be both etherial and earthly, the reason of which I have explained in the note to that hymn, it is obvious why the Stars, being celestial, are here said to consist of *heaven* and *earth*.

VIII.

TO THE SUN.

THE FUMIGATION FROM FRANKINCENSE AND MANNA.

Hear, golden Titan, whose eternal eye
With matchless sight illumines all the sky.
Native, unwearied in diffusing light,
And to all eyes the object of delight:
Lord of the Seasons, beaming light from far,
Sonorous, dancing [19] in thy four-yok'd car.
With thy right hand the source of morning light,
And with thy left the father of the night [20].

---

[19] Proclus, in his most elegant hymn to the Sun, says of this divinity:

Σης δ'απο μειλιχοδωρος αλεξικακου Θιασειης
Παιηων βλαστησειν, εην δ'επιτασσειν υγιειην,
Πλησας αρμονιης παναπημονος ευρεα κοσμον. i. e.

"From thy bland *dance* repelling deadly ill,
Salubrious Pæon blossoms into light,
Health far diffusing, and th' extended world
With streams of harmony innoxious fills."

[20] The hand is a symbol of power. Hence Proclus, in Theol. Plat. lib. 6, p. 380, says that those who are skilled in divine concerns attribute two hands to the Sun; denominating one the right hand, the other the left.

Agile and vig'rous, venerable Sun,
Fiery and bright around the heav'ns you run,
Foe to the wicked, but the good man's guide,
O'er all his steps propitious you preside.
With various-sounding golden lyre 'tis thine
To fill the world with harmony divine.
Father of ages, guide of prosp'rous deeds,
The world's commander, borne by lucid steeds.
Immortal Jove[21], flute-playing, bearing light,
Source of existence, pure and fiery bright;
Bearer of fruit, almighty lord of years,
Agile and warm, whom ev'ry power reveres.
Bright eye, that round the world incessant flies,
Doom'd with fair fulgid rays to set and rise;
Dispensing justice, lover of the stream,
The world's great master, and o'er all supreme.
Faithful defender[22], and the eye of right,
Of steeds the ruler, and of life the light:

---

[21] As all the celestial spheres are replete with processions from all the supermundane deities, which processions are the satellites of the leading divinities of these spheres, as we have shown in the Introduction, the reason is obvious why the sun is called Jupiter, a solar Jupiter being one of his attendants. But there is also another reason for this appellation. For what Jupiter is in the intellectual that the Sun is in the sensible order of things. Hence Proclus, in Theol. Plat. p. 289, calls the sun $\beta\alpha\sigma\iota\lambda\epsilon\upsilon\varsigma$ $\tau\upsilon$ $\pi\alpha\nu\tau\upsilon\varsigma$, *the king of the universe*.

[22] Proclus, in Tim. lib. 5, informs us, in the words of Orpheus, $\upsilon\tau\iota$ $\eta\lambda\iota\upsilon\nu$ $\mu\epsilon\nu$ $\iota\pi\iota\sigma\tau\eta\sigma\epsilon$ $\tau\upsilon\iota\varsigma$ $\upsilon\lambda\upsilon\iota\varsigma$ υ $\delta\eta\mu\iota\upsilon\upsilon\rho\gamma\upsilon\varsigma$, $\kappa\alpha\iota$

With sounding whip four fiery steeds you guide,
When in the glittering car of day you ride,
Propitious on these mystic labours shine,
And bless thy suppliants with a life divine.

IX.

TO THE MOON [23].

THE FUMIGATION FROM AROMATICS.

HEAR, Goddess queen, diffusing silver light,
Bull-horn'd [24], and wand'ring thro' the gloom of Night.

φυλακα αυτον ετευξε, κελευσε τε πασιν ανασσειν, "That the Demiurgus established the Sun over the whole of the universe, and fashioned him as its *guardian*, commanding him to govern all things."

[23] The Moon is called in this hymn both σεληνη and μηνη, the former of which words signify the Moon in the language

---

[24] We are informed by Porphyry, in his treatise De Antro Nymph. that the ancient priests of Ceres, called the Moon, who is the queen of generation, i. e. of the sublunary regions, a bull. He adds, "And Taurus is the exaltation of the Moon." And Olympiodorus, in his MS. Commentary on the Gorgias of Plato, says that the Moon, according to ancient theologists, is drawn by two bulls; by two, on account of her increase and diminution; but by *bulls*, because as these till the ground, so the Moon governs all those parts which surround the earth.

With stars surrounded, and with circuit wide
Night's torch extending, through the heav'ns you ride:

of the Gods; and the latter is the appellation given to her by men, as is evident from the following Orphic fragment:

Μησατο δ' αλλην γαιαν απειριτον, ηντε Σεληνην
Αθανατοι κληζουσιν, επιχθονιοι δε τε Μηνην.
Η πολλ' ουρε εχει, πολλ' αστεα, πολλα μελαθρα.

i. e. "But he (Jupiter) fabricated another boundless earth, which the Immortals call Selene, but men Mene; which has many mountains, many cities, many houses." This difference of names arises from the difference between divine and human knowledge. For, as it is well observed by the Platonic philosophers, as the knowledge of divine natures is different from that of partial souls like ours; so with respect to names, some are divine, exhibiting the whole essence of that which is named; but others are human, which only partially unfold their signification. On this difference of names, Proclus, in the last chapter of his first book on the Theology of Plato, admirably remarks as follows: "The first, most principal, and truly divine names are established in the Gods themselves. But the second names, which are imitations of the first, and which subsist intellectually, are of an allotment pertaining to dæmons. And again, we may say that those names which are the third from the truth, which are logically devised, and which receive the ultimate resemblance of divine natures, are unfolded by scientific men, at one time energizing divinely, and at another intellectually, and generating moving images of their inward spectacles. For as the demiurgic intellect establishes resemblances about matter of the first forms contained in himself, and produces temporal images of things eternal, divisible images of things indivisible, and adumbrated images as it were of true beings, after the same manner I think the science that is with us representing intellectual production fabricates resemblances of other things, and also

Female and male [25], with silv'ry rays you shine,
And now full-orb'd, now tending to decline.

of the Gods themselves, representing that which is void
of composition in them, through composition; that which
is simple, through variety; and that which is united, through
multitude; and thus fashioning names ultimately exhibits
images of divine natures. For it generates every where
name as if it were a statue of the Gods. And as the
theurgic art through certain symbols calls forth the exuberant and unenvying goodness of the Gods into the illumination of artificial statues; thus also the intellectual science
of divine concerns, by the compositions and divisions of
sounds, unfolds the occult essence of the Gods." See more
on this subject in the additional notes to my translation of
the Cratylus of Plato.

[25] Ficinus, on the Theology of Plato (lib. 4, p. 128), has
the following remarkable passage, most probably derived
from some MS. Commentary of Proclus, or some other of
the latter Platonists; for unfortunately he does not acquaint
us with the source of his information. "The professors (says
he) of the Orphic theology consider a twofold power in souls,
and in the celestial orbs; the one consisting in knowledge,
the other in vivifying and governing the orb with which that
power is connected. Thus, in the orb of the earth, they call
the gnostic power Pluto, but the other Proserpine. In water
they denominate the former power Ocean, and the latter
Tethys. In air, that thundering Jove, and this Juno. In
fire, that Phanes, and this Aurora. In the soul of the lunar
sphere, they call the gnostic power Liknitan Bacchus, the
other Thalia. In the sphere of Mercury, that Bacchus
Silenus, this Euterpe. In the orb of Venus, that Lysius
Bacchus, this Erato. In the sphere of the Sun, that Trietericus Bacchus, this Melpomene. In the orb of Mars, that
Bassareus Bacchus, this Clio. In the sphere of Jupiter,
that Sebazius, this Terpsichore. In the orb of Saturn, that

Mother of ages, fruit-producing Moon,
Whose amber orb makes Night's reflected noon:
Lover of horses, splendid queen of night,
All-seeing pow'r, bedeck'd with starry light,
Lover of vigilance, the foe of strife,
In peace rejoicing, and a prudent life:
Fair lamp of Night, its ornament and friend,
Who giv'st to Nature's works their destin'd end[26].

Amphietus, this Polymnia. In the eighth sphere, that
Pericionius, this Urania. But in the soul of the world they
call the gnostic power Bacchus Eribromus, but the animating
power Calliope. From all which the Orphic theologists
infer, that the particular epithets of Bacchus are compared
with those of the Muses, for the purpose of informing us
that the powers of the Muses are, as it were, intoxicated
with the nectar of divine knowledge; and in order that we
may consider the nine Muses, and nine Bacchuses, as re-
volving round one Apollo, that is about the splendour of one
invisible Sun." The greater part of this passage is preserved by Gyraldus in his Syntagma de Musis, and by
Natales Comes in his Mythology, but without mentioning
the original author. As in each of the celestial spheres,
therefore, the soul of the ruling deity is of the female, and
the intellect is of the male characteristic, it is by no means
wonderful that the Moon is called in this hymn "*female
and male.*"

[26] Proclus, in Plat. Theol. p. 403, informs us respecting
Diana, who among the mundane divinities is the Moon,
" That she excites all physical productive powers or forms
into energy, and that she gives perfection to the imperfection of matter. Hence both Theologists and Socrates, in
the Theætetus, call her *Lucina*, as the inspective guardian
of physical progression and generation." παντας κινουσα

Queen of the stars [27], all-wise Diana, hail!
Deck'd with a graceful robe and ample veil.
Come, blessed Goddess, prudent, starry, bright,
Come, moony-lamp, with chaste and splendid light,
Shine on these sacred rites with prosp'rous rays,
And pleas'd accept thy suppliants' mystic praise.

τους φυσικους λογους εις ενεργειαν, και το αυτοτελες (lege το ατελες) της υλης τελειουσα· διο και Λοχιαν αυτην οιτε θεολογοι, και ο εν Θεαιτητῳ Σωκρατης καλουσιν, ως της φυσικης προοδου, και γεννησεως εφορον. The epithet in the Orphic hymn is τελεσφορος, i. e. *bringing to a perfect end*.

[27] In the original αστραρχη. This appellation was first given to the Moon by the Phœnicians, as we are informed by Herodian. This Goddess likewise was called by the Africans Urania. Vide Selden. de Diis Syriis, p. 248.

X.

TO NATURE[28].

THE FUMIGATION FROM AROMATICS.

Nature, all-parent, ancient and divine,
O much mechanic mother, art is thine;
Heav'nly, abundant, venerable queen,
In ev'ry part of thy dominions seen.

---

[28] Nature, as we are informed by Proclus, in Tim. p. 4, is the last of the demiurgic causes of this sensible world, and the boundary of the extent of incorporeal essenses, and is full of productive powers and forms, through which she directs and governs mundane beings. And she is a goddess indeed in consequence of being deified; but she has not immediately the subsistence of a deity. For, says he, we call divine bodies Gods, as being the statues of Gods. He adds, But she governs the whole world by her powers, containing the heavens in the summit of herself, but ruling over generation [or the sublunary realms] through the heavens; and every where weaving together partial natures with wholes. Being however such, she proceeds from the vivific Goddess [Rhea]. For [according to the Chaldean Oracle] 'Immense Nature is suspended from the back of the Goddess;' from whom all life is derived, both that which is intellectual, and that which is inseparable from the subjects of its government. Hence, being suspended from thence, she pervades without impediment through, and inspires all things; so that through her the most inanimate beings participate of a certain soul, and such things as are

Untam'd, all taming, ever splendid light,
All ruling, honour'd, and supremely bright.
Immortal, first-born, ever still the same,
Nocturnal, starry, shining, powerful dame.
Thy feet's still traces in a circling course,
By thee are turn'd, with unremitting force.

corruptible remain perpetually in the world, being held together by the causes of forms which she contains."

Hence Nature is represented in this hymn as *turning the still traces of her feet with a swift whirling*. For since she is the last of the demiurgic causes, her operations aptly symbolize with the traces of feet. But the reason why the epithets of *much-mechanic, artist, connecting, all-wise providence*, &c. are given to Nature, which evince her agreement with Minerva, is because, as Proclus in the above extract informs us, she every where *weaves* together partial natures with wholes. Hence, according to the Orphic theology, as we also learn from Proclus, Minerva fashioned the variegated veil of Nature, from that wisdom and virtue of which she is the presiding deity. Nature, therefore, from her connecting and uniting power, and from her plenitude of seminal productive powers, has an evident agreement with Minerva; whose divine arts, according to the Orphic theology, reduce whatever is discordant and different in the universe into union and consent.

Again, it is well observed by Simplicius, in his Commentary on the Second Book of Aristotle's Physics, " that one of the conceptions which we form of Nature is, that it is *the character of every thing*, and that in consequence of this, we employ the name of it in all things, and do not refuse to say the *nature* of soul, of intellect, and even of deity itself." Nature, therefore, as indicating the *characteristic* or hyparxis of divinity, is in perfect conformity to the symbolical theology of Orpheus, said to be without a father, and at the

Pure ornament of all the Pow'rs divine,
Finite and infinite alike you shine[29];
To all things common, and in all things known,
Yet incommunicable and alone.
Without a father of thy wondrous frame,
Thyself the father whence thy essence came;
Mingling, all-flourishing, supremely wise,
And bond connective of the earth and skies.
Leader, life-bearing queen, all various nam'd,
And for commanding grace and beauty fam'd.

same time the father of her own being. For all the Gods, according to this theology, though they proceed by an *αρρητος εκφανσις* or *ineffable unfolding into* light from the first principle of things, yet at the same time are *αυτοτελεις υποστασεις*, or self-perfect, and self-produced essences. And when Nature in this hymn is said to be *incommunicable* and *alone*, this must be considered as indicating the characteristic of the great first principle of all. For so far as *the principle of all things* he is *incommunicable;* since it is impossible that there should be more than one principle of *all things.*

[29] Philolaus, as we are informed by Diogenes Laertius, published a treatise on Nature, of which this was the beginning: φυσις δε εν τῳ κοσμῳ αρμοχθη εξ απειρων τε και περαινοντων, και ολος κοσμος, και τα εν αυτῳ παντα, i. e. "Nature and the whole world, and whatever. it contains, are aptly connected together from things *infinite* and *finite*." Hence Socrates, in the Philebus of Plato, says, "that all beings consist of *bound* and *infinity*, and that these two intelligible principles were produced the first of all things by the highest God." Proclus, in Plat. Theol. Lib. 3, p. 132, cites the above passage of Philolaus.

Justice, supreme in might, whose general sway
The waters of the restless deep obey.
Etherial, earthly, for the pious glad,
Sweet to the good, but bitter to the bad:
All-wise, all-bounteous, provident, divine,
A rich increase of nutriment is thine;
And to maturity whate'er may spring,
You to decay and dissolution bring.
Father of all, great nurse, and mother kind,
Abundant, blessed, all-spermatic mind:
Mature, impetuous, from whose fertile seeds
And plastic hand this changing scene proceeds.
All-parent pow'r, in vital impulse seen,
Eternal, moving, all-sagacious queen.
By thee the world, whose parts in rapid flow,
Like swift descending streams, no respite know[30],
On an eternal hinge, with steady course,
Is whirl'd with matchless, unremitting force.

---

[30] As the world has an extended and composite essence, and is on this account continually separated from itself, it can alone be connected by a certain indivisible power imparted to it by divinity. Again, since from a natural appetite, it is perpetually moved in an orderly manner towards good, the nature of such an appetite and motion must originate from a divine intellect and goodness. But since, from its material imperfection, it cannot receive the whole of divine infinity at once, but in a way adapted to its temporal nature; hence it can only derive it gradually and partially, as it were by drops, in a momentary succession. So that the corporeal world is in a continual state of flowing

Thron'd on a circling car, thy mighty hand
Holds and directs the reins of wide command:
Various thy essence, honour'd, and the best,
Of judgment too, the general end and test.
Intrepid, fatal, all-subduing dame,
Life everlasting, Parca, breathing flame.
Immortal Providence, the world is thine,
And thou art all things, architect divine.
O, blessed Goddess, hear thy suppliants' pray'r,
And make their future life thy constant care;
Give plenteous seasons and sufficient wealth,
And crown our days with lasting peace and health.

and formation, but never possess real being; and is like the image of a lofty tree seen in a rapid torrent, which has the appearance of a tree without the reality; and which seems to endure perpetually the same, yet is continually renewed by the continual renovation of the stream.

XI.

TO PAN [31].

THE FUMIGATION FROM VARIOUS ODOURS.

Strong past'ral Pan, with suppliant voice I call,
Heav'n, sea, and earth, the mighty queen of all,
Immortal fire; for all the world is thine,
And all are parts of thee, O pow'r divine.
Come, blessed Pan, whom rural haunts delight,
Come, leaping, agile, wand'ring, starry light.
Thron'd with the Seasons, Bacchanalian Pan,
Goat-footed, horn'd, from whom the world began;
Whose various parts, by thee inspir'd, combine
In endless dance and melody divine.
In thee a refuge from our fears we find,
Those fears peculiar to the humankind.

---

[31] Pan, as we are informed by Damascius, first subsists at the extremity of the *intelligible* order, being there no other than the celebrated Protogonus or Phanes; but, according to his mundane subsistence, he is the monad or summit of all the local Gods and dæmons. In the statues of him his upper parts resemble those of a man, but his lower parts those of a brute [viz. of a goat] indicating by this, that in the universe rationality has dominion over irrationality. As, therefore, according to his first subsistence, he is the primary exemplar of the universe; the reason is obvious why in this hymn he is celebrated as *all things*.

Thee, shepherds, streams of water, goats rejoice,
Thou lov'st the chase and Echo's secret voice:
The sportive Nymphs thy ev'ry step attend,
And all thy works fulfill their destin'd end.
O all-producing pow'r, much-fam'd, divine,
The world's great ruler, rich increase is thine.
All-fertile Pæan, heavenly splendour pure,
In fruits rejoicing, and in caves[32] obscure.
True serpent-horned Jove[33], whose dreadful rage,
When rous'd, 'tis hard for mortals to assuage.

[32] A cave, as we are informed by Porphyry De Antr. Nymph. is an apt symbol of the material world; since it is agreeable at its first entrance on account of its participation of form, but is involved in the deepest obscurity to the intellectual eye, which endeavours to discern its dark foundation. Hence, like a cave, its exterior and superficial parts are pleasant, but its interior parts are obscure; and its very bottom darkness itself.

[33] Pan, as we have already observed, first subsists at the extremity of the intelligible order, and is the same with Protogonus or Phanes. This being the case, in the intellectual order he is analogous to Jupiter the Demiurgus, by whom, according to Orpheus, Phanes was absorbed. Hence, as Jupiter is said to be the mingler of all things by Orpheus, as we learn from Io. Diac. Allegor. in Hesiod, p. 305, horns are an occult symbol of the mingling power of the Demiurgus of the world. For the literal meaning of the word κεραστης, used in this hymn, is horned serpent; and one of the heads of Protogonus is that of a serpent. And the word κεραστης is, as Gesner observes, derived from the verb κεραννυμι, to mingle.

By thee the earth wide-bosom'd, deep and long,
Stands on a basis permanent and strong.
Th' unwearied waters of the rolling sea,
Profoundly spreading, yield to thy decree.
Old Ocean, too, reveres thy high command,
Whose liquid arms begird the solid land.
The spacious air, whose nutrimental fire
And vivid blasts the heat of life inspire;
The lighter frame of fire, whose sparkling eye
Shines on the summit of the azure sky,
Submit alike to thee, whose gen'ral sway
All parts of matter, various form'd, obey.
All natures change thro' thy protecting care,
And all mankind thy lib'ral bounties share;
For these, where'er dispers'd thro' boundless space,
Still find thy providence support their race.
Come, Bacchanalian, blessed pow'r, draw near,
Enthusiastic Pan, thy suppliants hear,
Propitious to these holy rites attend,
And grant our lives may meet a prosp'rous end;
Drive panic fury too, wherever found,
From humankind to earth's remotest bound.

XII.

TO HERCULES.

Hear, strenuous Hercules, untam'd and strong,
To whom grand works and powerful hands belong,
Titan untam'd, rejoicing and benign,
Of various forms, eternal and divine.
Father of Time, the theme of gen'ral praise,
Ineffable, adored in various ways,
Magnanimous, in divination skill'd,
And in th' athletic labours of the field.
'Tis thine, strong archer, all things to devour,
Supreme, all-helping, all-producing pow'r.
To thee mankind as their deliv'rer pray,
Whose arm can chase the savage tribes away.
Unweary'd, earth's best blossom [34], offspring fair,
To whom calm peace and peaceful works are dear.

---

[34] Since, according to Orpheus, there is an intellectual which is the source of the sensible world; the former containing in a primary and causal manner what the latter comprehends secondarily and sensibly; hence the former contains an intellectual heaven and earth, not like the material existing in place, and conversant with the circulations of time; but subsisting immaterially in the stable essence of eternity. In this divine world another sun and moon and stars shine with intellectual light; for every thing there is perfectly lucid, light continually mingling with

38   THE MYSTICAL HYMNS

Self-born, with primogenial fires[35] you shine,
And various names, and strength of heart are thine:

light. From this heaven and earth resident in the *intellectual* Phanes, Orpheus, according to Proclus, derives the sublunary orders of the Gods; and among these (vid. Procl. in Tim. p. 295), he enumerates the following progeny of the intellectual earth. " She produced seven beautiful pure virgins with voluble eyes, and seven sons, all of them kings, and covered with downy hair. The daughters are Themis and prudent Tethys, and fair-haired Mnemosyne and blessed Thea; together with Dione, having an illustrious form, and Phœbe, and Rhea the mother of king Jupiter. Moreover, this illustrious earth generated celestial sons, which are also surnamed Titans, because they took revenge on the great starry Heaven; and these are Cæus, and great Cræus, and robust Phorcys, and Saturn, and Ocean, and Hyperion, and Jupiter." Now as Hercules is celebrated in this hymn as the Sun, and the Sun is the same with Hyperion, the reason is obvious why Hercules is called " Earth's best blossom." And we shall find that Saturn, in the following hymn, is called " blossom of Earth;" and Themis, in hymn 79, " Young blossom of Earth;" and the Titans, in hymn 37, " the illustrious progeny of Heaven and Earth." Again,

Phanes, as we are informed by Athenagoras, is denominated by Orpheus Hercules and Time. Hence, we see the reason why Hercules in this hymn is said " to shine with primogenial fires;" since he is no other than *Protogonus* in the intelligible and intellectual worlds, and the Sun in the sensible world. Or in conformity to the Orphic theory mentioned in the Introduction, it may be said that he is celebrated with solar epithets, as being one of the satellites of the Sun.

[35] In the editions of Gesner and Hermann we have in this place βολισιν, and in the edition of Eschenbach φολισι; but

Thy mighty head supports the morning light,
And bears, untam'd, the silent gloomy night;
From east to west, endu'd with strength divine,
Twelve glorious labours to absolve is thine;
Supremely skill'd, thou reign'st in heav'n's abodes,
Thyself a God, amidst th' immortal Gods.
With arms unshaken, infinite, divine,
Come, blessed pow'r, and to our rites incline;
The mitigations of disease convey,
And drive disastrous maladies away.
Come, shake the branch with thy almighty arm,
Dismiss thy darts, and noxious fate disarm.

the true reading is, I have no doubt, φλογισι, conformably to the above translation. Scaliger also in his version has "*Ignibu'* primigenis florens."

XIII.

TO SATURN.

THE FUMIGATION FROM STORAX.

ETHERIAL father, mighty Titan[36], hear,
Great sire of Gods and men, whom all revere;
Endu'd with various counsel, pure and strong,
To whom increase and decrement belong.
Hence matter's flowing forms thro' thee that die,
By thee restor'd, their former place supply.
The world immense in everlasting chains,
Strong and ineffable thy pow'r contains;
Father of vast eternity, divine,
O mighty Saturn, various speech is thine;
Blossom of earth and of the starry skies,
Husband of Rhea, and Prometheus wise.
Obsteteric pow'r and venerable root,
From which the various forms of being shoot;
No parts peculiar can thy pow'r enclose,
Diffus'd thro' all, from which the world arose.
O best of beings, of a subtle mind,
Propitious hear, to suppliant pray'rs inclin'd;
The sacred rites benevolent attend,
And grant a blameless life, a blessed end.

[36] Saturn is one of the Titans produced by the intellectual Earth, as is evident from Note 34, on the hymn to Hercules.

XIV.

TO RHEA[37].

THE FUMIGATION FROM AROMATICS.

Illustrious Rhea, to my pray'r incline,
Daughter of various-form'd Protogonus[38] divine,

[37] Rhea, according to the Orphic and Platonic theology, is one of the zoogonic or vivific principles of the universe, having a maternal rank among the paternal orders, i. e. between Saturn, who subsists at the summit, and Jupiter, who subsists at the extremity of the intellectual order. Hence, she calls forth the causes latent in Saturn to the procreation of the universe; and definitely unfolds all the genera of the Gods. So that she is filled from Saturn, with an intelligible and prolific power, which she imparts to Jupiter, the Demiurgus of the universe; filling his essence with a vivific abundance. Since this Goddess then is a medium between the two intellectual parents of the universe, Saturn and Jupiter, the former of which collects intellectual multitude into one, but the latter scatters and divides it;— hence, says Proclus (in Plat. Theol. p. 266), this Goddess produces in herself the demiurgic causes of the universe; but imparts her diffusive power abundantly to secondary natures. On this account Plato assimilates her prolific abundance to the flowing of waters; signifying nothing more by the word *flowing* than that fontal power by which she contains in transcendent union the divisible rivers of life. Proclus likewise in p. 267 of the same work informs us, that this Goddess, according to Orpheus, when considered as united to Saturn by the most exalted part of her essence, is called Rhea; but considered as producing Jupiter, and together with Jupiter unfolding the total and partial orders of the Gods, she is called Ceres.

[38] Phanes or Protogonus, as we are informed by Proclus

Who driv'st thy sacred car with speed along,
Drawn by fierce lions, terrible and strong.
Mother of Jove, whose mighty arm can wield
Th' avenging bolt and shake the dreadful shield.
Brass-sounding [39], honour'd, Saturn's blessed queen,
Drum-beating, fury-loving, of a splendid mien.

in Tim. p. 291, not only subsists among the intelligible, but also among the intellectual Gods; in the demiurgic order, and among the supermundane and mundane Gods. And in a similar manner Night and Heaven: for the peculiarities of these are received through all the middle orders. Hence, as Rhea is one of the progeny of the intellectual Earth resident in Phanes, as we have before observed, the reason is obvious why she is said in this hymn to be the daughter of Protogonus. The Phanes, however, and Earth, from which Rhea proceeds, subsist in that divine order which is denominated by the Chaldean theologists νοητος και νοερος, *intelligible and at the same time intellectual*, and is celebrated by Plato in the Phædrus under the appellation of *Heaven*. This order, as subsisting between the intelligible and intellectual orders, participates of the former, and is κατα σχεσιν through proximity and alliance, the latter. Hence it is *primarily* intellectual.

[39] The reason why Rhea is here called *brass-sounding*, and in the next line *drum-beating*, is in consequence of the enthusiastic energy of which she is the source. Hence, says Porphyry, in his Epistle to Anebo: " Some of those who suffer a mental alienation energize enthusiastically on hearing certain cymbals or drums, or a certain modulated sound, such as those who are Corybantically inspired, those who are possessed by Sabazius, and those who are inspired by the mother of the Gods." On this passage, Iamblichus (De Myst. Sect. III. Cap. 9) beautifully observes as follows: " That music is of a motive nature, and is adapted to excite the affections, and that the melody of pipes produces or

Thou joy'st in mountains and tumultuous fight,
And mankind's horrid howlings thee delight.

heals the disordered passions of the soul, changes the temperaments or dispositions of the body, and by some melodies causes a Bacchic fury, but by others occasions this fury to cease; and likewise how the differences of these accord with the several dispositions of the soul, and that unstable and variable melody is adapted to ecstasies, such as are the melodies of Olympus, and others of the like kind; all these appear to me to be adduced in a way foreign to enthusiasm. For they are physical and human, and the work of our art; but nothing whatever of a divine nature in them presents itself to the view.

"We must rather, therefore, say that sounds and melodies are appropriately consecrated to the Gods. There is also an alliance in these sounds and melodies to the proper orders and powers of the several Gods, to the motions in the universe itself, and to the harmonious sounds which proceed from the motions. Conformably therefore to such like adaptations of melodies to the Gods, the Gods themselves become present. For there is not any thing which intercepts; *so that whatever has but a casual similitude to directly participates of them.* A perfect possession likewise immediately takes place, and a plenitude of a more excellent essence and power." In Cap. 10, also he observes, "that since the power of the Corybantes is in a certain respect of a guardian and efficacious nature, and that of Sabazius appropriately pertains to Bacchic inspiration, the purifications of souls, and the solutions of ancient divine anger, on this account the inspirations of them entirely differ from each other. With respect, however, to the Mother of the Gods, those who are precedaneously inspired by her are women; but the males that are thus inspired are very few in number, and such as are more effeminate. This enthusiasm, however, has a *vivific* and replenishing power, on which account also it in a remarkable degree

War's parent, mighty, of majestic frame,
Deceitful saviour[40], liberating dame.

differs from all other mania." In this extract the reason
why Iamblichus says that the enthusiasm of the Mother of
the Gods has a *vivific* power is because she is a vivific
Goddess, or the source of life to all things, being the same
with Rhea. See more on this most interesting subject in
my translation of this work of Iamblichus on the Mysteries.

[40] When Jupiter was born (says the fable), his mother
Rhea, in order to deceive Saturn, gave him a stone wrapped
in swaddling bands, in the place of Jupiter, at the same
time informing Saturn that what she gave him was her
offspring. Saturn immediately devoured the stone; and
Jupiter, who was *secretly* educated, at length obtained the
government of the world. Such is the fable, as narrated by
Phurnutus. (Vid. Opusc. Mythol. p. 147.) According to
Phurnutus also, this fable adumbrates the creation of the
world. "For at that time (says he) Nature [i. e. Jupiter
according to him] was then nourished in the world, and at
length prevailed. But the stone devoured by Saturn is the
earth, alluding to its firmly occupying the middle place:
for beings could not be permanent, without such a foundation for their support. From this all things are produced,
and derive their proper aliment." This explanation of the
fable by Phurnutus, who was a Stoic philosopher, is very
foreign from its true meaning. But the Stoics, though they
greatly excelled in ethics, were very deficient in theology.
The true solution of the fable, therefore, is only to be
derived from Platonic, which are the same with the Orphic
dogmas; and conformably to these, the development of the
fable is as follows: Rhea is the fontal cause of all life, and
is the middle deity of the intellectual triad, which consists
of Saturn, Rhea, and Jupiter. But the peculiarities of the
vivific order are (as Proclus demonstrates in MS. Comment.
in Parmenidem) motion and permanency, the former unfold-

Mother of Gods and men, from whom the earth
And spacious heav'ns derive their glorious birth.
Th' etherial gales, the deeply spreading sea,
Goddess, aerial-form'd, proceed from thee.
Come, pleas'd with wand'rings, blessed and divine,
With peace attended on our labours shine;
Bring rich abundance; and, wherever found,
Drive dire disease to earth's remotest bound.

ing into light the fountains of life, and the latter firmly establishing this life exempt from its proper rivers. The same thing is also demonstrated by him in Plat. Theol. lib. v. Damascius also, περι αρχων, observes, Τῃ Ρεᾳ η ογδοας προσηκει, ως επι παν κινηθεισῃ κατα τας διαιρεσεις, και ουδεν ηττον εστωσῃ παγιως και κυβικως. i. e. "The ogdoad, or number eight, pertains to Rhea, as being moved to every thing, according to divisions or distributions of her essence, and nevertheless at the same time she remains firmly and cubically established." Damascius uses the word *cubically*, because eight is a cubic number. Rhea, therefore, considered as firmly establishing her offspring Jupiter, in Saturn, who exists in unproceeding union, is fabulously said to have given Saturn a stone instead of Jupiter, the stone indicating the *firm* establishment of Jupiter in Saturn. For all divine progeny, at the same time that they proceed from, abide in their causes. And the *secret* education of Jupiter indicates his being nurtured in the intelligible order: for this order is denominated by ancient theologists *occult*.

XV.

TO JUPITER[41].

THE FUMIGATION FROM STORAX.

O JOVE, much-honour'd, Jove supremely great,
To thee our holy rites we consecrate,
Our pray'rs and expiations, king divine,
For all things to produce with ease thro' mind[42] is
    thine.
Hence mother Earth and mountains swelling high
Proceed from thee, the deep and all within the sky.
Saturnian king, descending from above,
Magnanimous, commanding, sceptred Jove;
All-parent, principle and end of all[43],
Whose pow'r almighty shakes this earthly ball;

---

[41] For a copious development of the nature of this divinity, see the additional notes.

[42] What I have here translated *thro' mind*, is in the original δια συν κεφαλην, as it appeared to me to be obvious, that by the head *mind* must be indicated, of which the head is the receptacle.

[43] Jupiter is *the principle* of all things in the universe, so far as he is the Demiurgus, but so far as he is the final cause, he is *the end of all*. Hence, too, Jupiter as the principle of the universe contains it in himself: for all things

Ev'n Nature trembles at thy mighty nod,
Loud-sounding, arm'd with light'ning, thund'ring
   God.

flow from their principle. In conformity to this, the following Orphic verses are cited by Proclus, in Tim. p. 95.

> Hence with the universe great Jove contains
> Extended ether, heav'n's exalted plains;
> The barren sea, wide-bosom'd earth renown'd,
> Ocean immense, and Tartarus profound;
> Fountains and rivers, and the boundless main,
> With all that Nature's ample realms contain,
> And Gods and Goddesses of each degree;
> All that is past, and all that e'er shall be,
> Occultly, and in fair connection lies
> In Jove's vast belly, ruler of the skies.

In the last line of these verses, *the belly* of Jupiter is indicative of all that subsists as a *middle* in the universe; the belly being the middle part of the body. So that the poet, by asserting that all things are contained in the belly of Jupiter, occultly signifies to us, that this deity is not only the beginning and end, but also the *middle* of all things, as comprehending all *middles* in himself. A certain modern, not having the smallest conception of what the Greek theologist meant by the belly of Jupiter, says, somewhere in his voluminous mythological treatise, in answer to one who rightly conceived that the latter part of the above Orphic lines contained a grand image of the maker of the universe, "that it excited no other idea of Jupiter than that of an enormous glutton."

In the same place also, Proclus cites other Orphic verses, which are likewise to be found in the Treatise de Mundo (ascribed to Aristotle); previous to which he observes, that the Demiurgus, being full of ideas, comprehended through these all things in himself, as the theologist Orpheus says.

Source of abundance, purifying king,
O various-form'd, from whom all natures spring;

With these verses I have connected others, conformably to the order of Stephens, Eschenbach, and Gesner, as follows:

> Jove is the first and last, high thund'ring king,
> Middle and head, from Jove all beings spring.
> In Jove the male and female forms combine,
> For Jove's a man, and yet a maid divine.
> Jove the strong basis of the earth contains,
> And the deep splendour of the starry plains.
> Jove is the breath of all; Jove's wondrous frame
> Lives in the rage of ever-restless flame.
> Jove is the sea's strong root, the solar light;
> And Jove's the moon, fair regent of the night.
> Jove is a king, by no restraint confin'd;
> And all things flow from Jove's prolific mind:
> One is the power divine, in all things known,
> And one the ruler absolute, alone.
> For in Jove's royal body all things lie,
> Fire, night and day, earth, water, and the sky;
> The first begetter's pleasing Love and Mind;
> These in his mighty body Jove confin'd.
> See how his beauteous head and aspect bright
> Illumine heav'n, and scatter boundless light!
> Round which his pendent golden tresses shine,
> Form'd from the starry beams, with light divine,
> On either side two radiant horns behold,
> Shap'd like a bull's, and bright with glitt'ring gold;
> And East and West in opposition lie,
> The lucid paths of all the Gods on high.
> His eyes the Sun and Moon with borrow'd ray;
> His mind is truth, unconscious of decay,
> Royal, etherial; and his ear refin'd
> Hears ev'ry voice and sounds of ev'ry kind.
> Thus are his head and mind immortal bright,
> His body boundless, stable, full of light.

Propitious hear my pray'r, give blameless health,
With peace divine, and necessary wealth.

> Strong are his members, with a force endu'd,
> Pow'rful to tame, but ne'er to be subdu'd.
> Th' extended region of surrounding air
> Forms his broad shoulders, back, and bosom fair;
> And thro' the world the ruler of the skies,
> Upborne on natal rapid pinions, flies.
> His sacred belly earth with fertile plains
> And mountains swelling to the clouds contains.
> His middle zone's the spreading sea profound,
> Whose roaring waves the solid globe surround.
> The distant realms of Tartarus obscure,
> Within Earth's roots, his holy feet secure;
> For these, Earth's utmost bounds, to Jove belong,
> And form his basis permanent and strong.
> Thus all things Jove within his breast conceal'd,
> And into beauteous light from thence reveal'd.

Jupiter, therefore, or the Demiurgus, is, according to Orpheus, all things, as containing in the unfathomable depths of his essence the causes of every thing which the sensible universe contains, these causes infinitely transcending the effects which they produce. Hence, by a causal priority, he is every thing which is contained in the sensible world. Pherecydes Syrus, also, conformably to this doctrine, says of Jupiter, as we learn from Kircher (in Œdip. Egypt. tom. ii. p. 89),

Ο Θεος εστι κυκλος, τετραγωνος, και δε τριγωνος
Κεινος δ' η γραμμη, κεντρον, και παντα προ παντων.

i. e. " Jove is a circle, trigon, and a square,
Centre and line, and all things before all."

Thus too, the ineffable principle of things is said be *all things prior to all*, not as containing all things multitudinously in itself, but as that from which all things are ineffably unfolded into light.

XVI.

TO JUNO[44].

THE FUMIGATION FROM AROMATICS.

O ROYAL Juno, of majestic mien,
Aerial-form'd, divine, Jove's blessed queen,
Thron'd in the bosom of cerulean air,
The race of mortals is thy constant care.
The cooling gales thy pow'r alone inspires,
Which nourish life, which ev'ry life desires.
Mother of show'rs and winds, from thee alone,
Producing all things, mortal life is known:
All natures share thy temp'rament divine,
And universal sway alone is thine.
With sounding blasts of wind, the swelling sea
And rolling rivers roar when shook by thee.
Come, blessed Goddess, fam'd almighty queen,
With aspect kind, rejoicing and serene.

[44] Juno is called by the Orphic theologists, as we are informed by Proclus, ζωογονος θεα, *the vivific Goddess;* an epithet perfectly agreeing with the attributes ascribed to her in this hymn. Proclus also in Plat. Theol. p. 483, says, " that Juno is the source of the procreation of the soul." See more concerning this divinity in the additional notes.

XVII.

TO NEPTUNE[45].

THE FUMIGATION FROM MYRRH.

Hear, Neptune, ruler of the sea profound,
Whose liquid grasp begirds the solid ground;
Who, at the bottom of the stormy main,
Dark and deep-bosom'd hold'st thy wat'ry reign.
Thy awful hand the brazen trident bears,
And Ocean's utmost bound thy will reveres.
Thee I invoke, whose steeds the foam divide,
From whose dark locks the briny waters glide;
Whose voice, loud sounding thro' the roaring deep,
Drives all its billows in a raging heap;
When fiercely riding thro' the boiling sea,
Thy hoarse command the trembling waves obey.
Earth-shaking, dark-hair'd God, the liquid plains
(The third division) Fate to thee ordains.
'Tis thine, cerulean dæmon, to survey,
Well-pleas'd, the monsters of the ocean play.
Confirm earth's basis, and with prosp'rous gales
Waft ships along, and swell the spacious sails;
Add gentle Peace, and fair-hair'd Health beside,
And pour abundance in a blameless tide.

[45] See the nature of this divinity unfolded in the additional notes.

XVIII.

TO PLUTO.

A HYMN.

Pluto, magnanimous, whose realms profound
Are fix'd beneath the firm and solid ground,
In the Tartarean plains remote from sight,
And wrapt for ever in the depths of night.
Terrestrial Jove [46], thy sacred ear incline,
And pleas'd accept these sacred rites divine.
Earth's keys [47] to thee, illustrious king, belong,
Its secret gates unlocking, deep and strong.
'Tis thine abundant annual fruits to bear,
For needy mortals are thy constant care.
To thee, great king, all-sov'reign Earth's assign'd,
The seat of Gods and basis of mankind.

---

[46] Pluto, says Proclus, in Plat. Theol. p. 368, is called *terrestrial Jupiter*, because he governs by his providence the earth and all it contains.

[47] Proclus, in the Excerpta from his Commentary on the Cratylus of Plato, informs us that initiators into the Mysteries, in order that sensibles might sympathize with the Gods, employed the shuttle as a signature of *separating*, a cup of *vivific*, a sceptre of *ruling*, and a KEY of *guardian power*. Hence Pluto, as the guardian of the earth, is here said to be the keeper of the earth's keys.

Thy throne is fix'd in Hades' dismal plains,
Distant, unknown to rest, where darkness reigns;
Where, destitute of breath, pale spectres dwell,
In endless, dire, inexorable hell;
And in dread Acheron, whose depths obscure,
Earth's stable roots eternally secure.
O mighty dæmon, whose decision dread,
The future fate determines of the dead,
With captive Proserpine, thro' grassy plains,
Drawn in a four-yok'd car with loosen'd reins,
Rapt o'er the deep, impell'd by love, you flew
Till Eleusina's city rose to view:
There, in a wondrous cave obscure and deep,
The sacred maid secure from search you keep,
The cave of Atthis, whose wide gates display
An entrance to the kingdoms void of day.
Of works unseen and seen thy power alone
To be the great dispensing source is known.
All-ruling, holy God, with glory bright,
Thee sacred poets and their hymns delight,
Propitious to thy mystics' works incline,
Rejoicing come, for holy rites are thine.

XIX.

TO THUNDERING JUPITER.

THE FUMIGATION FROM STORAX.

O FATHER Jove, who shak'st with fiery light
The world, deep-sounding from thy lofty height.
From thee proceeds th' etherial lightning's blaze,
Flashing around intolerable rays.
Thy sacred thunders shake the blest abodes,
The shining regions of th' immortal Gods.
Thy pow'r divine the flaming lightning shrouds
With dark investiture in fluid clouds.
'Tis thine to brandish thunders strong and dire,
To scatter storms, and dreadful darts of fire;
With roaring flames involving all around,
And bolts of thunder of tremendous sound.
Thy rapid dart can raise the hair upright,
And shake the heart of man with wild affright.
Sudden, unconquer'd, holy, thund'ring God,
With noise unbounded flying all abroad;
With all-devouring force, entire and strong,
Horrid, untam'd, thou roll'st the flames along.
Rapid, etherial bolt, descending fire,
The earth, all-parent, trembles at thine ire;

The sea all-shining, and each beast, that hears
The sound terrific, with dread horror fears:
When Nature's face is bright with flashing fire,
And in the heav'ns resound thy thunders dire.
Thy thunders white the azure garments tear,
And burst the veil of all-surrounding air.
O Jove, all-blessed, may thy wrath severe,
Hurl'd in the bosom of the deep appear,
And on the tops of mountains be reveal'd,
For thy strong arm is not from us conceal'd.
Propitious to these sacred rites incline,
And to thy suppliants grant a life divine,
Add royal health, and gentle peace beside,
With upright reas'ning for a constant guide.

XX.

TO JUPITER

As the Primary Cause of Lightning.

THE FUMIGATION FROM FRANKINCENSE AND MANNA.

I CALL the mighty, holy, splendid, light,
Aerial, dreadful-sounding, fiery-bright,
Flaming, etherial light, with angry voice,
Lightning thro' lucid clouds with crashing noise.
Untam'd, to whom resentments dire belong,
Pure, holy pow'r, all-parent, great and strong:
Come, and benevolent these rites attend,
And grant the mortal life a pleasing end.

XXI.

TO THE CLOUDS.

THE FUMIGATION FROM MYRRH.

Aerial Clouds, thro' heav'ns resplendent plains
Who wander, parents of prolific rains;
Who nourish fruits, whose wat'ry frames are hurl'd,
By winds impetuous, round the mighty world.
Loud-sounding, lion-roaring, flashing fire,
In Air's wide bosom bearing thunders dire:
Impell'd by each sonorous stormy gale,
With rapid course along the skies ye sail.
With gentle gales your wat'ry frames I call,
On mother Earth with fruitful show'rs to fall.

XXII.

TO TETHYS [48].

THE FUMIGATION FROM FRANKINCENSE AND MANNA.

Tethys I call, with eyes cerulean bright,
Hid in a veil obscure from human sight:
Great Ocean's empress, wand'ring thro' the deep,
And pleas'd, with gentle gales, the earth to sweep;
Whose ample waves in swift succession go,
And lash the rocky shore with endless flow:
Delighting in the sea serene to play,
In ships exulting, and the wat'ry way.
Mother of Venus, and of clouds obscure,
Great nurse of beasts, and source of fountains pure.
O venerable Goddess, hear my pray'r,
And make benevolent my life thy care;
Send, blessed queen, to ships a prosp'rous breeze,
And waft them safely o'er the stormy seas.

[48] See the nature of this divinity unfolded in the additional notes.

XXIII.

TO NEREUS.

THE FUMIGATION FROM MYRRH.

O THOU who dost the roots of Ocean keep
In seats cerulean, dæmon of the deep,
With fifty nymphs (attending in thy train,
Fair virgin artists) glorying thro' the main:
The dark foundation of the rolling sea,
And Earth's wide bounds belong, much-fam'd, to thee.
Great dæmon, source of all, whose pow'r can make
The sacred basis of blest Ceres shake,
When blust'ring winds in secret caverns pent,
By thee excited, struggle hard for vent.
Come, blessed Nereus, listen to my pray'r,
And cease to shake the earth with wrath severe;
Send to thy mystics necessary wealth,
With gentle peace, and ever tranquil health.

XXIV.

TO THE NEREIDS.

THE FUMIGATION FROM AROMATICS.

DAUGHTERS of Nereus, resident in caves
Merg'd deep in ocean, sporting thro' the waves;
Fifty inspir'd Nymphs, who thro' the main
Delight to follow in the Triton's train,
Rejoicing close behind their cars to keep;
Whose forms half wild are nourish'd by the deep,
With other Nymphs of different degree,
Leaping and wand'ring thro' the liquid sea.
Bright, wat'ry dolphins, sonorous and gay,
Well-pleas'd to sport with bacchanalian play;
Nymphs beauteous-ey'd, whom sacrifice delights,
Give plenteous wealth, and *bless our mystic rites;*
For you at first disclosed the rites divine,
Of holy Bacchus and of Proserpine,
Of fair Calliope, from whom I spring,
And of Apollo bright, the Muses' king.

XXV.

TO PROTEUS[49].

PROTEUS I call, whom Fate decrees to keep
The keys which lock the chambers of the deep;
First-born, by whose illustrious pow'r alone
All Nature's principles were clearly shown.
Pure sacred matter to transmute is thine,
And decorate with forms all-various and divine.
All-honour'd, prudent, whose sagacious mind
Knows all that was and is of ev'ry kind,
With all that shall be in succeeding time,
So vast thy wisdom, wondrous and sublime:
For all things Nature first to thee consign'd,
And in thy essence omniform confin'd.
O father, to thy mystics' rites attend,
And grant a blessed life a prosp'rous end.

---

[49] Proteus, says Proclus, in Plat. Repub. p. 97, though inferior to the primary Gods, is immortal; and though not a deity, is a certain angelic intellect of the order of Neptune, comprehending in himself all the forms of things generated in the universe.

XXVI.

TO EARTH[50].

THE FUMIGATION FROM EVERY KIND OF SEED, EXCEPT BEANS AND AROMATICS.

O MOTHER Earth, of Gods and men the source,
Endu'd with fertile, all-destroying force;
All-parent, bounding, whose prolific pow'rs
Produce a store of beauteous fruits and flow'rs.
All-various maid, th' immortal world's strong base,
Eternal, blessed, crown'd with ev'ry grace;
From whose wide womb as from an endless root,
Fruits many-form'd, mature, and grateful shoot.
Deep-bosom'd, blessed, pleas'd with grassy plains,
Sweet to the smell, and with prolific rains.
All-flow'ry dæmon, centre of the world,
Around thy orb the beauteous stars are hurl'd
With rapid whirl, eternal and divine,
Whose frames with matchless skill and wisdom shine.
Come, blessed Goddess, listen to my pray'r,
And make increase of fruits thy constant care;
With fertile Seasons in thy train draw near,
And with propitious mind thy suppliants hear.

[50] According to the Orphic theology, Earth is the mother of every thing of which Heaven is the father. See the additional notes.

XXVII.

TO THE MOTHER OF THE GODS.

THE FUMIGATION FROM A VARIETY OF ODORIFEROUS SUBSTANCES.

Mother of Gods, great nurse of all, draw near,
Divinely honour'd, and regard my pray'r.
Thron'd on a car, by lions drawn along,
By bull-destroying lions, swift and strong,
Thou sway'st the sceptre of the pole divine [51],
And the world's middle seat, much fam'd, is thine.
Hence earth is thine, and needy mortals share
Their constant food, from thy protecting care.
From thee at first both Gods and men arose;
From thee the sea and ev'ry river flows.
Vesta and source of wealth thy name we find
To mortal men rejoicing to be kind;
For ev'ry good to give thy soul delights.
Come, mighty pow'r, propitious to our rites,
All-taming, blessed, Phrygian Saviour, come,
Saturn's great queen, rejoicing in the drum.

---

[51] The Mother of the Gods is the same with Rhea; and Proclus, in the second book of his Commentary on Euclid, informs us, *that the pole of the world is called by the Pythagoreans the seal of Rhea.*

Celestial, ancient, life-supporting maid,
Inspiring fury; give thy suppliant aid;
With joyful aspect on our incense shine,
And pleas'd, accept the sacrifice divine.

XXVIII.

TO MERCURY [52].

THE FUMIGATION FROM FRANKINCENSE.

HERMES, draw near, and to my pray'r incline,
Angel of Jove, and Maia's son divine;
Prefect of contests, ruler of mankind,
With heart almighty, and a prudent mind.
Celestial messenger of various skill,
Whose pow'rful arts could watchful Argus kill.

---

[52] Proclus, in his admirable Commentary on the First Alcibiades, of which two excellent editions have been recently published by Cousin and Creuzer, gives us the following information respecting Mercury, which as the reader will easily perceive greatly elucidates some parts of this hymn. "Mercury is *the source of invention;* and hence he is said to be the son of Maia; because *search*, which is implied by *Maia*, leads invention into light. He bestows too *mathesis* on souls, by unfolding the will of his father Jupiter; and this he accomplishes, as the angel or messenger of Jupiter. He is likewise the inspective guardian of *gymnastic exercises;* and hence *hermæ*, or carved statues of

With winged feet 'tis thine thro' air to course,
O friend of man, and prophet of discourse:
Great life-supporter, to rejoice is thine
In arts gymnastic, and in fraud divine.
With pow'r endu'd all language to explain,
Of care the loos'ner, and the source of gain.
Whose hand contains of blameless peace the rod,
Corucian, blessed, profitable God.
Of various speech, whose aid in works we find,
And in necessities to mortals kind.
Dire weapon of the tongue, which men revere,
Be present, Hermes, and thy suppliant hear;
Assist my works, conclude my life with peace,
Give graceful speech, and memory's increase.

Mercury, were placed in the Palæstræ; of *music*, and hence he is honoured as λυραιος, the *lyrist* among the celestial constellations; and of *disciplines*, because the invention of geometry, reasoning, and language is referred to this God. He presides, therefore, over every species of erudition, leading us to an intelligible essence from this mortal abode, governing the different herds of souls, and dispersing the sleep and oblivion with which they are oppressed. He is likewise the supplier of recollection, the end of which is a genuine intellectual apprehension of divine natures."

XXIX.

TO PROSERPINE.

A HYMN.

DAUGHTER of Jove, Persephone divine,
Come, blessed queen, and to these rites incline:
Only-begotten [53], Pluto's honour'd wife,
O venerable Goddess, source of life:
'Tis thine in earth's profundities to dwell,
Fast by the wide and dismal gates of hell.
Jove's holy offspring, of a beauteous mien,
Avenging Goddess, subterranean queen.
The Furies' source, fair-hair'd, whose frame proceeds
From Jove's ineffable and secret seeds.
Mother of Bacchus, sonorous, divine,
And many-form'd, the parent of the vine.
Associate of the Seasons, essence bright,
All-ruling virgin, bearing heav'nly light.
With fruits abounding, of a bounteous mind,
Horn'd, and alone desir'd by those of mortal kind.
O vernal queen, whom grassy plains delight,
Sweet to the smell, and pleasing to the sight:

---

[53] Proclus, in Tim. lib. 2, p. 139, says, " that the theologist [Orpheus] is accustomed to call Proserpine *only-begotten.*" Και γαρ ο Θεολογος την Κορην μουνογενειαν ειωθε προσαγορευειν. See the additional notes.

Whose holy form in budding fruits we view,
Earth's vig'rous offspring of a various hue:
Espous'd in autumn [54], life and death alone
To wretched mortals from thy pow'r is known:
For thine the task, according to thy will,
Life to produce, and all that lives to kill [55].
Hear, blessed Goddess, send a rich increase
Of various fruits from earth, with lovely Peace:
Send Health with gentle hand, and crown my life
With blest abundance, free from noisy strife;
Last in extreme old age the prey of Death,
Dismiss me willing to the realms beneath,
To thy fair palace and the blissful plains
Where happy spirits dwell, and Pluto reigns.

[54] "The rape of Proserpine, says Sallust (De Diis et Mundo, cap. 4) is fabled to have taken place about the opposite equinox; and this rape signifies the descent of souls." περι γουν την εναντιαν ισημεριαν η της Κορης αρπαγη μυθολογειται γενεσθαι, ο δη καθοδος εςι των ψυχων. According to Lydus De Mensibus, the festival of Proserpine was celebrated on the sixth of the Nones of October. Hence the reason is obvious why Proserpine is said in this hymn to have been espoused in autumn.

[55] Proclus, in Plat. Theol. p. 371, informs us, that according to the Eleusinian mysteries, Proserpine, together with Pluto, governs terrestrial concerns, and the recesses of the earth; and that she supplies the extreme parts of the universe with life, and imparts soul to those who by her power are rendered inanimate and dead. This is perfectly conformable to what is said in the above hymn.

XXX.

TO BACCHUS[56].

THE FUMIGATION FROM STORAX.

Bacchus I call loud-sounding and divine,
Inspiring God, a twofold shape is thine:
Thy various names and attributes I sing,
O firstborn, thrice begotten, Bacchic king.
Rural, ineffable, two-form'd, obscure,
Two-horn'd, with ivy crown'd, and Euion[57] pure:
Bull-fac'd and martial, bearer of the vine,
Endu'd with counsel prudent and divine:
Omadius, whom the leaves of vines adorn,
Of Jove and Proserpine occultly born
In beds ineffable; all-blessed pow'r,
Whom with triennial off'rings men adore.
Immortal dæmon, hear my suppliant voice,
Give me in blameless plenty to rejoice;
And listen gracious to my mystic pray'r,
Surrounded with thy choir of nurses fair.

---

[56] See the additional notes.

[57] So called from the voice of the Bacchants.

XXXI.

TO THE CURETES.

A HYMN.

LEAPING Curetes, who with dancing feet
And circling measures armed footsteps beat:
Whose bosoms Bacchanalian furies fire,
Who move in rhythm to the sounding lyre:
Who traces deaf when lightly leaping tread,
Arm-bearers, strong defenders, rulers dread:
Fam'd Deities the guards of Proserpine[58],
Preserving rites mysterious and divine:
Come, and benevolent this hymn attend,
And with glad mind the *herdsman's* life defend.

---

[58] The Corybantes, who in the *supermundane* are the same as the Curetes in the *intellectual* order, are said by Proclus, in Plat. Theol. lib. 6, p. 383, " to be the guards of Proserpine." And in Hymn xxxviii, the Curetes are celebrated as being also the Corybantes; in consequence of both these triads being of a guardian characteristic, and subsisting in profound union with each other.

XXXII.

TO PALLAS[59].

A HYMN.

Only-begotten, noble race of Jove,
Blessed and fierce, who joy'st in caves to rove:
O warlike Pallas, whose illustrious kind,
Ineffable, and effable we find:
Magnanimous and fam'd, the rocky height,
And groves, and shady mountains thee delight:
In arms rejoicing, who with furies dire
And wild the souls of mortals dost inspire.

---

[59] The supermundane vivific triad consists (as we are informed by Proclus in Plat. Theol. p. 371) of three *zoogonic* monads; and these are Diana, Proserpine, and Minerva. "And of these (says he) the highest or first is arranged according to *hyparxis* [i. e. the summit of essence]; the second according to *power*, which is definitive of life; and the third according to *vivific intellect*. Theologists, also, are accustomed to call the first *Coric Diana*; the second *Proserpine*; and the third *Coric Minerva*. I mean that they are thus denominated by the primary leaders of the Grecian theology. For by the Barbarians, likewise [i. e. the Chaldean theologists], the same things are manifested through other names. For they call the first monad *Hecate*; the middle monad *Soul*; and the third *Virtue*." Conformably to this, Psellus, in his Exposition of the Chaldaic Dogmas, says: των δε ζωογονων αρχων, η μεν ακροτης Εκατη καλειται·

OF ORPHEUS.

Gymnastic virgin of terrific mind,
Dire Gorgon's bane, unmarried, blessed, kind:
Mother of arts, impetuous; understood
As fury by the bad, but wisdom by the good.
Female and male, the arts of war are thine,
O much-form'd, dragoness[60], inspir'd, divine:
O'er the Phlegrean giants[61], rous'd to ire,
Thy coursers driving with destruction dire.

η δε μεσοτης, ψυχη αρχικη· η δε περατωσις, αρετη αρχικη. i. e. " Of the zoogonic principles, the summit is called *Hecate;* the middle, *ruling Soul;* and the extremity, *ruling Virtue.*" The supermundane order is also called by Proclus αρχικη, because the divinities of which it consists are *principles* and *rulers*.

The reason, therefore, is obvious why Minerva in this hymn is said *to delight in caves, rocks, groves, and shady mountains;* for this arises from her union with Diana. And hence it appears, that Runkenius was mistaken in asserting that these epithets were misplaced. We may likewise hence see the reason why, in line thirteen, Minerva is called "*female* and *male,*" as well as the Moon; and why the Moon in the hymn to her is called πανσοφε κουρη, " *all-wise virgin.*"

[60] It is easy to perceive the agreement between Minerva, who is characterized by divine wisdom and providence, and a dragon; since, according to Phurnutus, a dragon is of a vigilant and guardian nature.

[61] As the fable of the giants is well known, but its real meaning is known only to a few, the following explanation of the battles of the Gods is inserted from p. 373 of the Fragments of the Commentary of Proclus on the Republic of Plato: " The divided progressions of all things and their

Sprung from the head of Jove, of splendid mien,
Purger of evils, all-victorious queen.

essential separations supernally originate from that division
of first operating causes [i. e. from bound and infinity],
which is perfectly arcane; and subsisting according to those
principles which are expanded above wholes, they dissent
from each other; some being suspended from the unifying
monad *bound*, and about this determining their subsistence,
but others receiving in themselves a never failing power
from that *infinity* which is generative of wholes, and is a
cause productive of multitude and progression, and about
this establishing their proper essence. Just, therefore, as
the first principles of things are separated from each other,
all the divine genera and true beings are divided from each
other, according to an orderly progression. Hence some of
them are the leaders of *union* to secondary natures, but
others impart the power of *separation;* some are the causes
of *conversion*, convolving the multitude of progressions to
their proper principles; but others *bound the progressions*,
and the subordinate *generation* from the principles. Again,
some supply a *generative abundance* to inferior natures, but
others impart an *immutable* and *undefiled purity;* some bind
to themselves the cause of *separate* good, but others of the
good which is *consubsistent* with the beings that receive it.
And thus in all the orders of being is such a contrariety of
genera diversified. Hence *permanency*, which establishes
things in themselves, is opposed to *efficacious powers*, and
which are full of *life* and *motion*. Hence, too, the kindred
communion of *sameness* receives a division according to
species opposite to the separations of *difference;* but the
genus of *similitude* is allotted an order contrary to *dissimilitude;* and that of *equality* to *inequality*, according to the
same analogy. Is it, therefore, any longer wonderful, if
the authors of fables, perceiving such contrariety in the
Gods themselves and the first of beings, obscurely signified
this to their pupils through battles? the divine genera, in-

Hear me, O Goddess, when to thee I pray,
With supplicating voice both night and day,

deed, being perpetually united to each other, but at the
same time containing in themselves the causes of the union
and separation of all things.

We may also, I think, adduce another mode of solution;
viz. that the Gods themselves are impartibly connascent
with each other, and subsist uniformly in each other, but
that their progressions into the universe, and their communications are separated in their participants, become
divisible, and are thus filled with contrariety; the objects
of their providential exertions not being able to receive in
an unmingled manner the powers proceeding from thence,
and without confusion their multiform illuminations. We
may likewise say, that the last orders which are suspended
from divine natures, as being generated remote from first
causes, and as being proximate to the subjects of their
government, which are involved in matter, participate themselves of all-various contrariety and separation, and partibly preside over material natures, minutely dividing those
powers which presubsist uniformly and impartibly in their
first operating causes. Such, then, and so many, being
the modes according to which the mystic rumours of theologists refer war to the Gods themselves:—other poets,
and those who have explained divine concerns through a
divinely inspired energy, have ascribed wars and battles
to the Gods according to the first of those modes we
related, in which the divine genera are divided conformably to the first principles of wholes. For those powers
which *elevate to causes* are, after a manner, opposed to those
that are *the sources of generation,* and the *connective* to the
separating; those that *unite* to those that *multiply* the progression of things; *total* genera to such as fabricate *partibly;*
and those which are *expanded above* to those that *preside
over* partial natures: and hence fables, concealing the truth,
assert that such powers fight and war with each other.

And in my latest hour give peace and health,
Propitious times, and necessary wealth,
And ever present be thy vot'ries aid,
O much implor'd, art's parent, blue-ey'd maid.

On this account, as it appears to me, they assert that the Titans were the antagonists of Bacchus, and the Giants of Jupiter. For union, indivisible energy, and a wholeness prior to parts * are adapted to those fabricators that have a subsistence prior to the world. But the Titans and Giants produce the demiurgic powers into multitude, divisibly administer the affairs of the universe, and are the proximate fathers of material natures."

Proclus, in his elegant hymn to Minerva, says of this victory of Minerva over the Giants:

> Η σοφιης πιτασασα Θεοσιβεας πυλωνας,
> Και χθονιων δαμασασα θεωμαχα φυλα γιγαντων.

i. e. "The God-trod gates of wisdom by thy hand
Are wide unfolded, and the daring band
Of earth-born giants, that in impious fight,
Strove with thy sire, were vanquish'd by thy might."

---

* *Whole* has a triple subsistence; for it is either prior to parts, i. e. is the *cause* of the parts which it contains; or it is the aggregate of parts; or it subsists in a part. See my translation of Proclus's Elements of Theology.

XXXIII.

TO VICTORY.

THE FUMIGATION FROM MANNA.

O POWERFUL Victory, by men desir'd,
With adverse breasts to dreadful fury fir'd,
Thee I invoke, whose might alone can quell
Contending rage and molestation fell.
'Tis thine in battle to confer the crown,
The victor's prize, the mark of sweet renown;
For thou rul'st all things, Victory divine!
And glorious strife, and joyful shouts are thine.
Come, mighty Goddess, and thy suppliant bless,
With sparkling eyes, elated with success;
May deeds illustrious thy protection claim,
And find, led on by thee, immortal fame.

XXXIV.

TO APOLLO.

THE FUMIGATION FROM MANNA.

Blest Pæan, come, propitious to my pray'r,
Illustrious pow'r, whom Memphian tribes revere,
Slayer of Tityus, and the God of health,
Lycorian Phœbus, fruitful source of wealth:
Spermatic, golden-lyr'd, the field from thee
Receives its constant rich fertility.
Titanic, Grunian[62], Smynthian, thee I sing,
Python-destroying[63], hallow'd, Delphian king:

---

[62] Grynæus, according to Strabo, lib. 13, is a town of Myrinæus, and is likewise a temple of Apollo, and a most ancient oracle and temple, sumptuously built of white stone.

[63] "Typhon, Echidna, and Python being the progeny of Tartarus and Earth, which is conjoined with Heaven, (says Olympiodorus in MS. Comment. in Phædon.) form, as it were, a certain Chaldaic triad, which is the inspective guardian of the whole of a disordered fabrication [i. e. of the fabrication of the last of things]." Οτι Ταρταρου και Γης της συζυγουσης τῳ Ουρανῳ, ο Τυφων, η Εχιδνα, ο Πυθων, οιον Χαλδαικη τις τριας εφορος της αтактους πασης δημιουργιας. And in another part of the same Commentary he says, " that Typhon is the cause of the all-various sub-

Rural, light-bearer, and the Muses' head,
Noble and lovely, arm'd with arrows dread:
Far-darting, Bacchian, twofold, and divine,
Pow'r far diffus'd, and course oblique is thine.
O Delian king, whose light-producing eye
Views all within, and all beneath the sky;
Whose locks are gold, whose oracles are sure,
Who omens good reveal'st, and precepts pure;
Hear me entreating for the human kind,
Hear, and be present with benignant mind;
For thou survey'st this boundless ether all,
And ev'ry part of this terrestrial ball
Abundant, blessed; and thy piercing sight
Extends beneath the gloomy, silent night;

terranean winds and waters, and of the violent motion of the other elements. But Echidna is a cause revenging and punishing rational and irrational souls; and hence the upper parts of her are those of a virgin, but the lower those of a serpent. And *Python* is the guardian of the whole of prophetic production. Though it will be better to say, that he is the cause of the disorder and obstruction pertaining to things of this kind. Hence, also, Apollo destroyed Python, in consequence of the latter being adverse [to the prophetic energy of the former]. Ο μεν Τυφων της παντοιας των υπογαων πνευματων και υδατων, και των αλλων τοιχειων βιαιου κινησεως αιτιος· η δε Αιχιδνα τιμωρος αιτια και κολαστικη λογικων τε και αλογων ψυχων· διο τα μεν ανω παρθενος· τα δε κατω εςιν οφεωδης· ο δε Πυθων φρουρος της μαντικης ολης αναδοσεως· αμεινον δε της περι ταυτα αταξιας τε και αντιφραξεως αιτιον λεγειν· διο και Απολλων αυτον αναιρει εναντιουμενον.

Beyond the darkness, starry-ey'd [64], profound,
The stable roots, deep-fix'd by thee, are found.

[64] *The starry-eyed darkness*, beyond which Apollo is here said to fix his roots, is the sphere of the fixed stars, the region immediately beyond which consists of the etherial worlds, which according to the Chaldeans are three. For they assert that there are seven corporeal worlds, one empyrean and the first; after this, three etherial, and then three material worlds, which last consist of the inerratic sphere, the seven planetary spheres, and the sublunary region. But that, according to the Orphic theology, there is an etherial world beyond the sphere of the fixed stars is evident from the following mystic particulars respecting the Oracle of Night, which are transmitted to us by Proclus in his admirable Commentary on the Timæus, p. 63 and p. 96. " The artificer of the universe (says he), prior to his whole fabrication, is said to have betaken himself to the Oracle of Night, to have been there filled with divine conceptions, to have received the principles of fabrication, and, if it be lawful so to speak, to have solved all his doubts. Night, too, calls upon the father Jupiter to undertake the fabrication of the universe; and Jupiter is said by the theologist [Orpheus] to have thus addressed Night:

Μαια θεων υπατη, Νυξ αμβροτε, πως ταδε φρασεις;
Πως δει μ'αθανατων αρχην κρατεροφρονα θεσθαι;
Πως δε μοι εν τι τα παντ' εςαι, και χωρις εκαςον;

i. e. O Nurse supreme of all the pow'rs divine,
 Immortal Night! how with unconquer'd mind
 Must I the source of the Immortals fix?
 And how will all things but as one subsist,
 Yet each its nature separate preserve?

To which interrogations the Goddess thus replies:

Αιθερι παντα περιξ αφατω λαβε· τω δ'ενι μεσσω

OF ORPHEUS.

The world's wide bounds, all-flourishing, are thine,
Thyself of all the source and end divine.

> Ουρανον, εν δε τε γαιαν απειριτον, εν δε θαλασσαν,
> Εν δε τε τειρεα παντα, τα τ'ουρανος εςεφανωτο.

i. e. All things receive enclos'd on ev'ry side,
   In Ether's wide, ineffable embrace;
   Then in the midst of Ether place the Heav'n,
   In which let Earth of infinite extent,
   The Sea, and Stars the crown of Heav'n be fixt.

We also learn from Psellus, that according to the Chaldeans there are two solar worlds; *one which is subservient* to the etherial profundity; the other zonaic, being one of the seven spheres. (See his concise Exposition of Chaldaic Dogmas.) And Proclus, in Tim. p. 264, informs us, " that according to the most mystic assertions, the *wholeness* of the Sun is in the supermundane order. For there a solar world and a total light subsist, as the Oracles of the Chaldeans affirm." Οι γε μυστικωτατοι των λογων, και την ολοτητα αυτου (solis) την εν τοις υπερκοσμιοις παραδεδωκασιν· εκει γαρ ο ηλιακος κοσμος, και το ολον φως, ως αι τε Χαλδαιων φημοι λεγουσι. These etherial worlds pertain to the supermundane order of Gods, in which the *wholeness* of the Sun subsists. But by the *wholeness* (ολοτης) Proclus means the sphere in which the visible orb of the Sun is fixed, and which is called a *wholeness*, because it has a perpetual subsistence, and comprehends in itself all the multitude of which it is the cause. Conformably to this, the Emperor Julian (in Orat. v. p. 334) says : " The orb of the Sun revolves in the starless, much above the inerratic sphere. Hence he is not the middle of the planets, but of the three worlds [i. e. of the three etherial worlds], according to the telestic hypothesis." Ο δισκος επι της αναστρου φερεται, πολυ της απλανους υψηλοτερας, και ουτω δε των μεν πλανωμενων ουκ εξει το μεσον, τριων δε των κοσμων κατα τας τελεστικας υποθεσεις. From all this, therefore, it

'Tis thine all Nature's music to inspire
With various-sounding, harmonizing lyre[65]:

is evident why Apollo in this hymn is said to fix his roots beyond the starry-eyed darkness; for this signifies that Gods are inserted by him in the etherial worlds; *roots* being indicative of *summits* (ακροτητες) and such, according to the Orphic and Chaldaic theologists, are the Gods. Hence Proclus (in MS. Comment. in Parmenid. lib. vi.) beautifully observes, " As trees by their summits are firmly established in the earth, and all that pertains to them is through this earthly; after the same manner divine natures are by their summits *rooted in the one*, and each of them is a unity and one, through an unconfused union with *the one itself*." καθαπερ γαρ τα δενδρα ταις εαυτων κορυφαις ενιδρυνται τῃ γῃ, και εϛι γηινα τα κατ'εκεινας, τον αυτον τροπον και τα θεια, ταις εαυτων ακροτησιν ενερριζωται τῳ ενι, και εκαϛον αυτων ενας εϛι καί εν, δια την προς το εν αϲυγχυτον ενωϲιν.

[65] Gesner well observes, in his notes on this hymn, that the comparison and conjunction of the musical and astronomical elements are most ancient; being derived from Orpheus and Pythagoras to Plato. The lyre of Apollo, however, is not only indicative of the harmony of the universe, of which this divinity is the source, but particularly adumbrates according to the Orphic and Pythagoric doctrine, the celestial harmony, or the melody caused by the revolutions of the celestial spheres. This harmony of the spheres is admirably unfolded by Simplicius in his Commentary on the second book of Aristotle's Treatise on the Heavens, as follows: " The Pythagoreans said, that an harmonic sound is produced from the motion of the celestial bodies; and they scientifically collected this from the analogy of their intervals; since not only the ratios of the intervals of the sun and moon, and Venus and Mercury, but also of the other stars, were discovered by them." Simplicius

Now the last string thou tun'st to sweet accord[66],
Divinely warbling, now the highest chord;

adds, " Perhaps the objection of Aristotle to this assertion
of the Pythagoreans may be solved as follows, according to
the philosophy of those men: all things are not commensurate with each other, nor is every thing sensible commensurate to every thing, even in the sublunary region. This
is evident from dogs, who scent animals at a great distance,
and which are not smelt by men. How much more, there-

---

[66] The following quotation from Nicomachus (Harm. lib.
i. p. 6) illustrates the meaning of the hypate and nete, or
the highest and lowest string, in the lyre of Apollo: " From
the motion of Saturn (says he) the most remote of the
planets, the appellation of the gravest sound, hypate, is
derived; but from the lunar motion, which is the lowest of
all, the most acute sound is called nete, or the lowest."
But Gesner observes, that a more ancient, and as it were
archetypal, appellation is derived from the ancient triangular lyre, a copy of which was found among the pictures
lately dug out of the ruins of Herculaneum; in which the
highest chord next to the chin of the musician is the longest,
and consequently (says he) the sound is the most grave.
Gesner proceeds in observing, that three seasons of the
year are so compared together in a musical ratio, that
hypate signifies the Winter, nete the Summer, and the
Dorian measure represents the intermediate seasons, Spring
and Autumn. Now the reason why the Dorian melody is
assigned to the Spring, is because that measure wholly consists in temperament and moderation, as we learn from
Plutarch in his Treatise De Musica. Hence it is with
great propriety attributed to the Spring, considered as
placed between Winter and Summer; and gratefully tempering the fervent heat of the one, and the intense cold of
the other.

Th' immortal golden lyre, now touch'd by thee,
Responsive yields a Dorian melody.

fore, in things which are separated by so great an interval
as those which are incorruptible from the corruptible, and
celestial from terrestrial natures, is it true to say that the
sound of divine bodies is not audible by terrestrial ears?
But if any one, like Pythagoras, who is reported to have
heard this harmony, should have his terrestrial body exempt
from him, and his luminous and celestial vehicle, and the
senses which it contains, purified, either through a good
allotment, or through probity of life, or through a perfection
arising from sacred operations, such a one will perceive
things invisible to others, and will hear things inaudible by
others. With respect to divine and immaterial bodies,
however, if any sound is produced by them, it is neither
percussive nor destructive, but it excites the powers and
energies of sublunary sounds, and perfects the sense which
is coordinate with them. It has also a certain analogy to
the sound which concurs with the motion of terrestrial
bodies. But the sound which is with us, in consequence of
the sonorific nature of the air, is a certain energy of the
motion of their impassive sound. If then, air is not passive
there, it is evident that neither will the sound which is
there be passive. Pythagoras, however, seems to have
said that he heard the celestial harmony, as understanding
the harmonic proportions in numbers, of the heavenly bodies,
and that which is audible in them. Some one, however,
may very properly doubt why the stars are seen by our
visive sense, but the sound of them is not heard by our ears?
To this we reply, that neither do we see the stars themselves; for we do not see their magnitudes, or their figures,
or their surpassing beauty. Neither do we see the motion
through which the sound is produced; but we see, as it
were, such an illumination of them as that of the light of the
sun about the earth, the sun himself not being seen by us.
Perhaps too, neither will it be wonderful, that the visive

All Nature's tribes to thee their diff'rence owe,
And changing seasons from thy music flow:
Hence, mix'd by thee in equal parts, advance
Summer and Winter in alternate dance;
This claims the highest, that the lowest string,
The Dorian measure tunes the lovely spring:
Hence by mankind Pan royal, two-horn'd nam'd,
Shrill winds emitting thro' the syrinx fam'd[67];

sense, as being more immaterial, subsisting rather according to energy than according to passion, and very much transcending the other senses, should be thought worthy to receive the splendour and illumination of the celestial bodies, but that the other senses should not be adapted for this purpose."

[67] According to the Pythagoric and Platonic theology, which is perfectly conformable to that of Orpheus, Apollo is in the supermundane what Jupiter is in the intellectual order. For as the former illuminates mundane natures with supermundane light, so the latter illuminates the supermundane order with intellectual light. Indeed, there is such a wonderful agreement between these two divinities, that the Cyprian priests, as we are informed by the Emperor Julian, in his most excellent Oration to the Sovereign Sun, raised common altars to Jupiter and the Sun. Hence we cannot wonder that the same thing is here asserted of Apollo which Orpheus elsewhere asserts of Jupiter. For Johan. Diaco. in Hesiod. Theog. quotes the following lines from Orpheus:

Ζευς δε τε παντων ετι θεος, παντων τε κεραςης,
Πνευμασι συριζων, φοναισι τε αερομικτοις.

i. e. "Jupiter is the God of all, and the mingler of all things, *emitting shrill sounds* from winds and air-mingled voices."

Since to thy care the figur'd seal's consign'd[66],
Which stamps the world with forms of ev'ry kind.
Hear me, blest pow'r, and in these rites rejoice,
And save thy mystics with a suppliant voice.

XXXV.

TO LATONA[69].

THE FUMIGATION FROM MYRRH.

Dark-veil'd Latona, much invoked queen,
Twin-bearing Goddess, of a noble mien;
Cæantis great, a mighty mind is thine,
Offspring prolific, blest, of Jove divine:
Phœbus proceeds from thee, the God of light,
And Dian fair, whom winged darts delight;

---

[66] In the preceding note we have mentioned the profound union which subsists between Apollo and Jupiter. As Jupiter, therefore, considered as the Demiurgus, comprehends in himself the archetypal ideas of all sensible forms, and what these forms are *intellectually* in the Demiurgus they are according to a *supermundane* characteristic in Apollo; hence the latter divinity, as well as the former, may be said to possess the figured seal, of which every visible species is nothing more than an impression.

[69] See the additional notes.

She in Ortygia's honour'd regions born,
In Delos he, which lofty mounts adorn.
Hear me, O qeeen, and fav'rably attend,
And to this *Telete divine afford a pleasing end.*

XXXVI.

TO DIANA.

THE FUMIGATION FROM MANNA.

HEAR me, Jove's daughter, celebrated queen,
Bacchian and Titan, of a noble mien:
In darts rejoicing, and on all to shine,
Torch-bearing Goddess, Dictynna divine.
O'er births presiding[70], and thyself a maid,
To labour pangs imparting ready aid:
Dissolver of the zone, and wrinkled care,
Fierce huntress, glorying in the silvan war:
Swift in the course, in dreadful arrows skill'd,
Wand'ring by night, rejoicing in the field:

---

[70] In the original λοχεια; and Proclus, in Plat. Theol. p. 403, informs us that this epithet is given by theologists to Diana, because she is the inspective guardian of natural progression and generation. See more concerning this divinity in the additional notes.

Of manly form, erect, of bounteous mind,
Illustrious dæmon, nurse of humankind:
Immortal, earthly, bane of monsters fell,
'Tis thine, blest maid, on woody mounts to dwell:
Foe of the stag, whom woods and dogs delight,
In endless youth you flourish fair and bright.
O universal queen, august, divine,
A various form, Cydonian pow'r, is thine.
Dread guardian Goddess, with benignant mind,
Auspicious come, to mystic rites inclin'd;
Give earth a store of beauteous fruits to bear,
Send gentle Peace, and Health with lovely hair,
And to the mountains drive Disease and Care.

XXXVII.

TO THE TITANS.

THE FUMIGATION FROM FRANKINCENSE.

O MIGHTY Titans, who from Heav'n and Earth
Derive your noble and illustrious birth,
Our fathers' sires, in Tartarus [71] profound
Who dwell, deep merg'd beneath the solid ground:
Fountains and principles from whom began
Th' afflicted miserable race of man [72]:

[71] "Tartarus (says Olympiodorus in MS. in Comment. on Phædon.) is a Deity who is the inspective guardian of the extremities of the world, just as Pontus [the sea] is the guardian of the middle, and Olympus of the summits of the universe. And these three are to be found not only in the sensible world, but also in the demiurgic intellect, in the supermundane, and the celestial order." Οτι ο Ταρταρος εστι τας εσχατιας του κοσμου επισκοπων, ως ο Ποντος τας μεσοτητας, ως ο Ολυμπος τας ακροτητας· εστιν ουν τρεις ευρειν ουκ εν τῳ αισθητῳ μονῳ τῳ δε κοσμῳ, αλλα και εν τῳ δημιουργικῳ νῳ, και εν τῳ κοσμῳ (lege υπερκοσμιῳ) διακοσμῳ, και εν τῳ ουρανιῳ.

[72] The reason why the Titans are said in this hymn to be the fountains and principles of mankind depends on the following arcane narration, for the sources of which I refer the reader to my Treatise on the Eleusinian and Bacchic Mysteries: Dionysius, or Bacchus, while he was yet a boy, was engaged by the Titans, through the stratagems of Juno, in a variety of sports, with which that period of life is so

Who not alone in earth's retreats abide,
But in the ocean and the air reside;
Since ev'ry species from your nature flows,
Which, all-prolific, nothing barren knows.
Avert your rage, if from th' infernal seats
One of your tribe should visit our retreats.

vehemently allured; and among the rest, he was particularly captivated with beholding his image in a mirror; during his admiration of which he was miserably torn in pieces by the Titans; who, not content with this cruelty, first boiled his members in water, and afterwards roasted them by the fire. But while they were tasting his flesh thus dressed, Jupiter, excited by the steam, and perceiving the cruelty of the deed, hurled his thunder at the Titans; but committed his members to Apollo, the brother of Bacchus, that they might be properly interred. And this being performed, Dionysius (whose heart during his laceration was snatched away by Minerva and preserved), by a new regeneration, again emerged, and he, being restored to his pristine life and integrity, afterwards filled up the number of the Gods. But in the mean time, from the exhalations formed from the ashes of the burning bodies of the Titans mankind were produced. The reader who is desirous of having a complete development of this fable will find it in my abovementioned Treatise on the Mysteries. Suffice it to say at present, in elucidation of this Orphic hymn, that (as Olympiodorus beautifully observes in MS. Comment. in Phædon.) we are composed from *fragments*, because through falling into generation, i. e. into the sublunary region, our life has proceeded into the most distant and extreme division; but from *Titannic fragments*, because the Titans are the ultimate artificers of things, and the most proximate to their fabrications. Of these Titans, Bacchus, or the mundane intellect, is the *monad*, or proximately exempt producing cause.

XXXVIII.

TO THE CURETES [73].

THE FUMIGATION FROM FRANKINCENSE.

BRASS-BEATING Salians, ministers of Mars,
Who wear his arms the instruments of wars;
Whose blessed frames, heav'n, earth, and sea compose,
And from whose breath all animals arose:
Who dwell in Samothracia's sacred ground,
Defending mortals through the sea profound.
Deathless Curetes, by your pow'r alone,
The greatest mystic rites to men at first were shown.
Who shake old Ocean thund'ring to the sky,
And stubborn oaks with branches waving high.
'Tis yours in glittering arms the earth to beat,
With lightly leaping, rapid, sounding feet;
Then ev'ry beast the noise terrific flies,
And the loud tumult wanders thro' the skies.

---

[73] The first subsistence of the Curetes is in the *intellectual* order, as we have before observed, in which they form a triad characterized by *purity*. They are also the guards of that order. But in the *supermundane* order, they are the Corybantes. Hence they are celebrated in this hymn as the Corybantes as well as the Curetes. As they are likewise celebrated as *Winds* in this hymn, it follows that in the sublunary region they are the divinities of such winds as are of a purifying nature.

The dust your feet excites, with matchless force
Flies to the clouds amidst their whirling course;
And ev'ry flower of variegated hue
Grows in the dancing motion form'd by you;
Immortal dæmons, to your pow'rs consign'd,
The task to nourish and destroy mankind,
When rushing furious with loud tumult dire,
O'erwhelm'd, they perish in your dreadful ire;
And live replenish'd with the balmy air,
The food of life, committed to your care.
When shook by you, the seas with wild uproar,
Wide-spreading, and profoundly whirling, roar.
The concave heav'ns with echo's voice resound,
When leaves with rustling noise bestrew the ground.
Curetes, Corybantes, ruling kings,
Whose praise the land of Samothracia sings;
Great Jove's assessors; whose immortal breath
Sustains the soul, and wafts her back from death;
Aerial-form'd, who in Olympus shine
The heavenly Twins [74] all-lucid and divine:
Blowing, serene, from whom abundance springs,
Nurses of seasons, fruit-producing kings.

---

[74] I have before observed that the Curetes and Corybantes
are celebrated in this hymn as one and the same, on account
of the profound union subsisting between the two. Hence
the progression of these two orders into the heavens forms
the constellation called the *Twins*.

XXXIX.

TO CORYBAS [75].

THE FUMIGATION FROM FRANKINCENSE.

THE mighty ruler of this earthly ball
For ever flowing, to these rites I call;
Martial and blest, unseen by mortal sight,
Preventing fears, and pleas'd with gloomy night:
Hence fancy's terrors are by thee allay'd,
All-various king, who lov'st the desert shade.
Each of thy brothers killing, blood is thine,
Twofold Curete, many-form'd, divine.
By thee transmuted, Ceres' body pure
Became a dragon's savage and obscure:
Avert thy anger, hear me when I pray,
And, by fix'd fate, drive fancy's fears away.

---

[75] Corybas is celebrated in this hymn as one of the Curetes; for he is called *Curete*. Perhaps, therefore, he is the last monad of the Curetic triad, and the extremity of every divine order being of a convertive nature, he is said to have killed each of his brothers. For slaughter, when applied to the Gods, signifies a segregation from secondary and a conversion to primary natures. Hence Corybas slaughters, i. e. converts his brothers to a superior order of Gods.

XL.

TO CERES.

THE FUMIGATION FROM STORAX.

O UNIVERSAL mother, Ceres fam'd,
August, the source of wealth[76], and various nam'd:
Great nurse, all-bounteous, blessed and divine,
Who joy'st in peace; to nourish corn is thine.
Goddess of seed, of fruits abundant, fair,
Harvest and threshing are thy constant care.
Lovely delightful queen, by all desir'd,
Who dwell'st in Eleusina's holy vales retir'd.
Nurse of all mortals, whose benignant mind
First ploughing oxen to the yoke confin'd;
And gave to men what nature's wants require,
With plenteous means of bliss, which all desire.

---

[76] The following Orphic verse, which is to be found in Diodorus Siculus, i. 12, perfectly accords with what is said in this and the first line,

Γη μητηρ παντων, Δημητηρ πλουτοδοτειρα.

i. e. " Earth, mother of all things, Ceres, source of wealth."

It must be observed that, according to the Orphic theology, Ceres is the same with Rhea, the vivific Goddess, who is the centre of the *intellectual* triad. See the additional notes.

In verdure flourishing, in glory bright,
Assessor of great Bacchus, bearing light:
Rejoicing in the reapers' sickles, kind,
Whose nature lucid, earthly, pure, we find.
Prolific, venerable, nurse divine,
Thy daughter loving, holy Proserpine.
A car with dragons yok'd 'tis thine to guide,
And, orgies singing, round thy throne to ride.
Only-begotten, much-producing queen,
All flowers are thine, and fruits of lovely green.
Bright Goddess, come, with summer's rich increase
Swelling and pregnant, leading smiling Peace;
Come with fair Concord and imperial Health,
And join with these a needful store of wealth.

XLI.

TO THE CERALIAN MOTHER.

THE FUMIGATION FROM AROMATICS.

CERALIAN queen, of celebrated name,
From whom both men and Gods immortal came;
Who widely wand'ring once, oppress'd with grief,
In Eleusina's valleys found'st relief,
Discovering Proserpine thy daughter pure
In dread Avernus, dismal and obscure;
A sacred youth while thro' the earth you stray,
Bacchus, attending leader of the way;
The holy marriage of terrestrial Jove
Relating, while oppress'd with grief you rove.
Come, much invok'd, and to these rites inclin'd,
Thy mystic suppliant bless, with fav'ring mind.

XLII.

TO MISA.

THE FUMIGATION FROM STORAX.

I CALL Thesmophorus[77], spermatic God,
Of various names, who bears the leafy rod:
Misa, ineffable, pure, sacred queen,
Twofold Iacchus[78], male and female seen.
Illustrious, whether to rejoice is thine
In incense offer'd in the fane divine[79];
Or if in Phrygia most thy soul delights,
Performing with thy mother sacred rites;
Or if the land of Cyprus is thy care,
Pleas'd with the well crown'd Cytheria fair;
Or if exulting in the fertile plains
With thy dark mother Isis, where she reigns,
With nurses pure attended, near the flood
Of sacred Egypt, thy divine abode:
Wherever resident, benevolent attend,
And in perfection these our labours end.

[77] i. e. The legislator.

[78] It is well known that Iacchus is a mystic appellation of Bacchus, so that Misa is Bacchus. Misa is also said to be both male and female, because this divinity comprehends in himself stable power and sameness, which are of a masculine characteristic, and the measures of life and prolific powers, which are feminine peculiarities. This mixture of the male and female in one and the same divinity is no unusual thing in the Orphic theology.

[79] i. e. The temple of Ceres Eleusina.

XLIII.

TO THE SEASONS[80].

THE FUMIGATION FROM AROMATICS.

DAUGHTERS of Jove and Themis, Seasons bright,
Justice, and blessed Peace, and lawful Right,
Vernal and grassy, vivid, holy pow'rs,
Whose balmy breath exhales in lovely flow'rs;

---

[80] " Sacred rumour (says Procl. in Tim. book iv. p. 247, of my translation of that work) venerates the invisible periods [subsisting under one first time], and which are the causes of those that are visible; delivering the divine names of Day and Night, and also the causes that constitute, and the invocations and self manifestations of Month and Year. Hence they are not to be surveyed superficially, but in divine essences, which the laws of sacred institutions and the oracles of Apollo order us to worship and honour, by statues and sacrifices, as histories inform us. When these also are reverenced, mankind are also supplied with the benefits arising from the periods of the *Seasons*, and of the other divinities in a similar manner; but a preternatural disposition of every thing about the earth is the consequence of the worship of these being neglected. Plato, likewise, in the Laws proclaims that all these are Gods, viz. the Seasons, Years, and Months, in the same manner as the Stars and the Sun; and we do not introduce any thing new by thinking it proper to direct our attention to the invisible powers of these prior to those that are visible."

Conformably to what Proclus here says, viz. " that a preternatural disposition of every thing about the earth is the

All-colour'd Seasons, rich increase your care,
Circling, for ever flourishing and fair:
Invested with a veil of shining dew,
A flow'ry veil delightful to the view:
Attending Proserpine, when back from night
The Fates and Graces lead her up to light;
When in a band harmonious they advance,
And joyful round her form the solemn dance.
With Ceres triumphing, and Jove divine,
Propitious come, and on our incense shine;
Give earth a store of blameless fruits to bear,
And make these novel mystics' life your care.

---

consequence of the worship of these powers being neglected." The inhabitants of Patros, in Egypt, said to the prophet Jeremiah, " But we will certainly do whatsoever thing goeth out of our mouth, to burn incense to the Queen of Heaven, and to pour out drink-offerings unto her, as we have done, we, and our fathers, our kings, and our princes, in the cities of Judah, and in the streets of Jerusalem: for *then had we plenty of victuals and were well, and saw no evil.* But since we left off to burn incense to the Queen of Heaven, and to pour out drink-offerings unto her, *we have wanted all things,* and have been consumed by the sword and by famine." Jeremiah, chap. 44, v. 17, 18.

XLIV.

TO SEMELE.

THE FUMIGATION FROM STORAX.

CADMEAN Goddess, universal queen,
Thee, Semele, I call, of beauteous mien;
Deep-bosom'd, lovely flowing locks are thine,
Mother of Bacchus, joyful and divine,
The mighty offspring, whom Jove's thunder bright
Forc'd immature, and fright'ned into light.
Born from the deathless counsels, secret, high,
Of Jove Saturnian, regent of the sky;
Whom Proserpine permits to view the light,
And visit mortals from the realms of night.
Constant attending on the sacred rites,
And feast triennial, which thy soul delights;
When thy son's wondrous birth mankind relate,
And secrets pure and holy celebrate.
Now I invoke thee, great Cadmean queen,
To bless thy mystics, lenient and serene.

XLV.

TO DIONYSIUS BASSAREUS TRIENNALIS[81].

A HYMN.

Come, blessed Dionysius, various-nam'd,
Bull-fac'd, begot from thunder, Bacchus fam'd.
Bassarian God, of universal might,
Whom swords and blood and sacred rage delight:
In heaven rejoicing, mad, loud-sounding God,
Furious inspirer, bearer of the rod:
By Gods rever'd, who dwell'st with humankind,
Propitious come, with much rejoicing mind.

[81] So called because his rites were performed every third year.

XLVI.

TO LICKNITUS[82] BACCHUS.

THE FUMIGATION FROM MANNA.

LICKNITAN Bacchus, bearer of the vine,
Thee I invoke to bless these rites divine:
Florid and gay, of Nymphs the blossom bright,
And of fair Venus, Goddess of delight.
'Tis thine mad footsteps with mad Nymphs to beat,
Dancing thro' groves with lightly leaping feet:
From Jove's high counsels nurst by Proserpine,
And born the dread of all the pow'rs divine.
Come, blessed God, regard thy suppliants' voice,
Propitious come, and in these rites rejoice.

[82] i. e. The Fan-bearer. Concerning Liknitus, and the following Bacchuses, see note 25, on the Moon.

XLVII.

TO BACCHUS PERICIONIUS[83].

THE FUMIGATION FROM AROMATICS.

BACCHUS Pericionius, hear my pray'r,
Who mad'st the house of Cadmus once thy care,
With matchless force his pillars twining round,
When burning thunders shook the solid ground,
In flaming, sounding torrents borne along,
Propt by thy grasp indissolubly strong.
Come, mighty Bacchus, to these rites inclin'd,
And bless thy suppliants with rejoicing mind.

[83] So called from περι, and κιονις, *a little pillar*.

XLVIII.

TO SABAZIUS[84].

THE FUMIGATION FROM AROMATICS.

HEAR me, illustrious father, dæmon fam'd,
Great Saturn's offspring, and Sabazius nam'd;
Inserting Bacchus, bearer of the vine,
And sounding God, within thy thigh divine,
That when mature, the Dionysian God
Might burst the bands of his conceal'd abode,
And come to sacred Tmolus, his delight,
Where Ippa[85] dwells, all beautiful and bright.

---

[84] "Many (says Plutarch, Symp. 4, 5, p. 671) even now call the Bacchuses *Sabbi*, and they utter this word when they celebrate the orgies of the God" [Bacchus]. Σαββους και νυν ετι πολλοι τους βαχχους καλουσι, και ταυτην αφιασι την φωνην, οταν οργιαζουσι τῳ θεῳ. "But the power of Sabazius (says Iamblichus de Myst. sect. iii. cap. x.) appropriately pertains to Bacchic inspiration, the purifications of souls, and the solutions of ancient divine anger." See the note on this passage in my translation of that work.

[85] "Ippa (says Proclus in Tim. lib. ii. p. 124), who is the soul of the universe, and is thus called by the theologist [Orpheus], perhaps because her intellectual conceptions are essentialized in the most vigorous motions, or perhaps on account of the most rapid lation of the universe, of which she is the cause,—placing a testaceous vessel on her head,

Blest Phrygian God, the most august of all,
Come aid thy mystics, when on thee they call.

and encircling the fig leaves that bind her temples with a dragon, receives Dionysius [or Bacchus]. For with the most divine part of herself, she becomes the receptacle of an intellectual essence, and receives *the mundane intellect*, which proceeds into her from the thigh of Jupiter. For there it was united with Jupiter; but proceeding from thence, and becoming participable by her, it elevates her to the intelligible, and to the fountain of her nature. For she hastens to the mother of the Gods, and to mount Ida [i. e. to the region of ideas, and an intelligible nature], from which all the series of souls is derived. Hence, also, Ippa is said to have received Dionysius when he was brought forth from Jupiter." Η μεν γαρ Ιππα του παντος ουσα ψυχη, και ουτω κεκλημενη παρα τῳ θεολογῳ, ταχα μεν οτι και εν ακμαιοταταις κινησεσιν εννοησεις αυτης ουσιωνται, ταχα δε και δια την οξυτατην του παντος φοραν ης εστιν η αιτια, λικιον (lege λικινον) επι της κεφαλης θεμενη, και δρακοντι αυτῳ περιστρεψασα, το κραδιαιον υποδεχεται Διονυσον· τῳ γαρ εαυτης θειοτατῳ, γινεται της νοερας ουσιας υποδοχη, και δεχεται τον εγκοσμιον νουν, ο δε απο του μηρου του Διος προεισιν εις αυτην· ην γαρ εκει συνηνωμενος, και προελθων, και μεθεκτος αυτῃ γενομενος, επι το νοητον αυτην αναγει, και την εαυτης πηγην· επειγεται γαρ προς την μητερα των θεων, και την Ιδην, αφ' ης πασα των ψυχων η σειρα· διο και συλλαμβανεσθαι και Ιππα λεγεται τικτοντι τῳ Διι.

XLIX.

TO IPPA.

THE FUMIGATION FROM STORAX.

GREAT nurse of Bacchus, to my pray'r incline,
For holy Sabus' secret rites are thine,
The mystic rites of Bacchus' nightly choirs,
Compos'd of sacred, loud-resounding fires.
Hear me, terrestrial mother, mighty queen,
Whether on Ida's holy mountain seen,
Or if to dwell in Tmolus thee delights,
With holy aspect come, and bless these rites.

L.

TO LYSIUS LENÆUS.

A HYMN.

Hear me, Jove's son, blest Bacchus, God of wine,
Born of two mothers, honour'd and divine;
Lysian Euion Bacchus, various-nam'd,
Of Gods the offspring, secret, holy, fam'd.
Fertile and nourishing, whose liberal care
Augments the fruit that banishes despair.
Sounding, magnanimous, Lenæan pow'r,
O various-form'd, medicinal, holy flow'r:
Mortals in thee repose from labour find,
Delightful charm, desir'd by all mankind.
Fair-hair'd Euion, Bromian, joyful God,
Lysian, insanely raging with the leafy rod.
To these our rites, benignant pow'r, incline,
When fav'ring men, or when on Gods you shine;
Be present to thy mystics' suppliant pray'r,
Rejoicing come, and fruits abundant bear.

LI.

TO THE NYMPHS[86].

THE FUMIGATION FROM AROMATICS.

Nymphs, who from Ocean fam'd derive your birth,
Who dwell in liquid caverns of the earth;
Nurses of Bacchus, secret-coursing pow'rs,
Fructiferous Goddesses, who nourish flow'rs:
Earthly, rejoicing, who in meadows dwell,
And caves and dens, whose depths extend to hell.
Holy, oblique, who swiftly soar thro' air,
Fountains, and dews, and winding streams your care,
Seen and unseen, who joy with wand'rings wide,
And gentle course thro' flow'ry vales to glide;

---

[86] Nymphs (says Hermeas, in Schol. in Phædrum.) are Goddesses who preside over regeneration, and are ministrant to Bacchus, the offspring of Semele. Hence they dwell near water, i. e. they ascend into generation [or the sublunary realms]. But this Bacchus [of whom they are the offspring] supplies the regeneration of the whole sensible world." Νυμφαι δε εισιν εφοροι θεαι της παλιγγενεσιας, υπουργοι του εκ Σεμελης Διονυσου· διο και παρα τῳ υδατι εισι, τουτεστι τῃ γενεσει επιβεβηκασιν· ουτος δε ο Διονυσος της παλιγγενεσιας υπαρχει παντος του αισθητου. He adds, "that some of them excite the irrational nature, others nature herself, and others preside over bodies."

With Pan exulting on the mountains' height,
Inspir'd, and stridulous, whom woods delight:
Nymphs od'rous, rob'd in white, whose streams exhale
The breeze refreshing, and the balmy gale;
With goats and pastures pleas'd, and beasts of prey,
Nurses of fruits, unconscious of decay.
In cold rejoicing, and to cattle kind,
Sportive, thro' ocean wand'ring unconfin'd.
O Nysian nymphs, insane, whom oaks delight,
Lovers of spring, Pæonian virgins bright;
With Bacchus and with Ceres hear my pray'r,
And to mankind abundant favour bear;
Propitious listen to your suppliant's voice,
Come, and benignant in these rites rejoice;
Give plenteous seasons and sufficient wealth,
And pour in lastings streams, continued health.

LII.

TO TRIETERICUS[87].

THE FUMIGATION FROM AROMATICS.

BACCHUS phrenetic [88], much nam'd, blest, divine,
Bull-horn'd, Lenæan, bearer of the vine;
From fire descended, raging, Nysian king,
From whom initial ceremonies spring.

[87] According to the fragment preserved by Ficinus, which we have before cited, Trietericus Bacchus is the gnostic power, or intellect of the Sun. Hence as the Sun is to the sensible world what Protogonus, or Phanes, is to the intellectual orders; for the latter illuminates those orders with intelligible, and the former the sensible world with supermundane light; in consequence of this analogy, the reason is obvious why Trietericus is called in this hymn Ericapæus, i. e. Protogonus; and also why he is said to be both the father and the offspring of Gods. For Protogonus is *intelligible intellect* (νους νοητος), and is the father of the Gods; and Trietericus, or the *solar intellect*, subsists causally in Protogonus, and proceeds from him and the intellectual orders of Gods. From his causal subsistence, therefore, in Protogonus, he is the father of the Gods; but as proceeding from them, he is their offspring.

[88] This word, and others of a similar kind, which literally signify insanity, are to be considered according to their recondite meaning, as indicative of a divinely inspired energy.

Liknitan Bacchus, pure and fiery bright,
Prudent, crown-bearer, wand'ring in the night;
Nurst in mount Mero, all-mysterious pow'r,
Triple, ineffable, Jove's secret flow'r:
Ericapæus, first-begotten nam'd,
Of Gods the father and the offspring fam'd.
Bearing a sceptre, leader of the choir,
Whose dancing feet phrenetic furies fire,
When the triennial band thou dost inspire,
Omadian, captor, of a fiery light,
Born of two mothers, Amphietus bright;
Love, mountain-wand'ring [89], cloth'd with skins of deer,
Apollo golden-ray'd [90], whom all revere.

[89] The reason why Trietericus Bacchus is called "*Love*" in this hymn is from the profound union subsisting between Phanes, or Protogonus, Jupiter, and Bacchus. For the first subsistence of Love, according to the Orphic theology, is in Phanes; and Phanes is *intelligible intellect*. But the intelligible order to which Phanes belongs being absorbed in the *superessential*, contains in itself intellect *causally*, and

[90] As according to the Orphic theology Trietericus is *the intellect of the Sun*, this divinity is with great propriety celebrated in this hymn as *Apollo golden-ray'd* (παιαν χρυσεγχης). But Hermann, not knowing who Trietericus is in the Orphic theology, substitutes θυρσεγχης for χρυσεγχης; conceiving that Trietericus is the same with Bacchus, or the *mundane intellect*. His words are, " Vocabulum παιαν postulat, ut nomen addatur, quo ab Apolline distinguatur Bacchus. Itaque pro χρυσεγχης reposui θυρσεγχης." Vid. Orphic. Hermann. p. 317.

Great annual God of grapes, with ivy crown'd,
Bassarian, lovely, virginlike, renown'd.
Come, blssed pow'r, regard thy mystics' voice,
Propitious come, and in these rites rejoice.

---

consequently is superior to *essential* intellect, and intellectual vision. Hence Love, according to his first subsistence, is said to be *blind*, as having a superintellectual energy. This being premised, it is no longer wonderful that Trietericus should be called Love. " For the theologist [Orpheus], says Proclus, in Tim. lib. ii. p. 102, long before us, celebrates the demiurgic cause in Phanes. *For there, as he says, the great Bromius, or all-seeing Jupiter, was, and antecedently existed;* in order that he might have as it were the fountains of the twofold fabrication of things. He also celebrates the paradigmatic cause [i. e. Phanes] in Jupiter. For again, he likewise is, as he says, *Metis the first generator, and much pleasing Love*. He is also continually denominated by him Dionysius, and Phanes, and Ericapæus. All the causes, therefore, participate of, and are in each other. παλαι γαρ ο θεολογος εν γε τῳ φανητι την δημιουργικην αιτιαν ανυμνησεν· εκει γαρ ην τε και προην ωσπερ εφη και αυτος, βρομιος τε μεγας και ζευς ο πανοπτης· και εν τῳ δια την παραδειγματικην· μητις γαρ αυ και ουτις εστιν ως φησι.

Και Μητις πρωτος γενετωρ, και Ερως πολυτερπης·

αυτος τε ο Διονυσος και φανης και ηρικεπαιος, συνεχως ονομαζεται· παντα αρα μετειληχην αλληλων τα αιτια, και εν αλληλοις εστιν.

LIII.

TO AMPHIETUS BACCHUS.

THE FUMIGATION FROM EVERY AROMATIC EXCEPT FRANKINCENSE.

TERRESTRIAL Dionysius, hear my pray'r,
Rise vigilant with Nymphs of lovely hair:
Great Amphietus Bacchus, annual God,
Who laid asleep in Proserpine's abode,
Her sacred seat, didst lull to drowsy rest
The rites triennial and the sacred feast;
Which rous'd again by thee, in graceful ring,
Thy nurses round thee mystic anthems sing;
When briskly dancing with rejoicing pow'rs,
Thou mov'st in concert with the circling hours.
Come blessed, fruitful, horned, and divine,
And on this sacred Telete propitious shine;
Accept the pious incense and the pray'r,
And make prolific holy fruits thy care.

LIV.

TO SILENUS, SATYRUS,
AND THE PRIESTESSES OF BACCHUS.

THE FUMIGATION FROM MANNA.

GREAT nurse of Bacchus, to my pray'r incline,
Silenus, honour'd by the pow'rs divine;
And by mankind at the triennial feast
Illustrious dæmon, reverenc'd as the best:
Holy, august, the source of lawful rites,
Phrenetic pow'r, whom vigilance delights;
Surrounded by thy nurses young and fair,
Naiads and Bacchic Nymphs who ivy bear,
With all thy Satyrs on our incense shine,
Dæmons wild-form'd, and bless the rites divine.
Come, rouse to sacred joy thy pupil king[91],
And Brumal Nymphs with rites Lenæan bring;
Our orgies shining thro' the night inspire,
And bless, triumphant pow'r, the sacred choir.

---

[91] Silenus is so called because he was the foster father or nurse of Bacchus.

LV.

TO VENUS.

A HYMN.

Heav'nly, illustrious, laughter-loving queen,
Sea-born, night-loving, of an awful mien;
Crafty, from whom necessity first came,
Producing, nightly, all-connecting dame.
'Tis thine the world with harmony to join[92],
For all things spring from thee, O pow'r divine.
The triple Fates are ruled by thy decree,
And all productions yield alike to thee:
Whate'er the heav'ns, encircling all, contain,
Earth fruit-producing, and the stormy main,
Thy sway confesses, and obeys thy nod,
Awful attendant of the Brumal God.
Goddess of marriage, charming to the sight,
Mother of Loves, whom banquetings delight;
Source of persuasion, secret, fav'ring queen,
Illustrious born, apparent and unseen;

---

[92] Venus, according to her first subsistence, ranks among the supermundane divinities. But she is the cause of all the harmony and analogy in the universe, and of the union of form with matter, connecting and comprehending the powers of all the mundane elements. See the additional notes.

Spousal, Lupercal, and to men inclin'd,
Prolific, most-desir'd, life-giving, kind.
Great sceptre-bearer of the Gods, 'tis thine
Mortals in necessary bands to join;
And ev'ry tribe of savage monsters dire
In magic chains to bind thro' mad desire.
Come, Cyprus-born, and to my pray'r incline,
Whether exalted in the heav'ns you shine,
Or pleas'd in od'rous Syria to preside,
Or o'er th' Egyptian plains thy car to guide,
Fashion'd of gold; and near its sacred flood,
Fertile and fam'd, to fix thy blest abode;
Or if rejoicing in the azure shores,
Near where the sea with foaming billows roars,
The circling choirs of mortals thy delight,
Or beauteous Nymphs with eyes cerulean bright,
Pleas'd by the sandy banks renown'd of old,
To drive thy rapid two-yok'd car of gold;
Or if in Cyprus thy fam'd mother fair,
Where nymphs unmarried praise thee ev'ry year,
The loveliest nymphs, who in the chorus join,
Adonis pure to sing, and thee divine.
Come, all-attractive, to my pray'r inclin'd,
For thee I call, with holy, reverent mind.

LVI.

TO ADONIS.

THE FUMIGATION FROM AROMATICS.

Much nam'd, and best of dæmons, hear my pray'r,
The desert loving, deck'd with tender hair;
Joy to diffuse, by all desir'd, is thine,
Much form'd, Eubulus, aliment divine.
Female and male, all-charming to the sight,
Adonis, ever flourishing and bright;
At stated periods doom'd to set and rise
With splendid lamp, the glory of the skies [93].
Two horn'd and lovely, reverenc'd with tears,
Of splendid form, adorn'd with copious hairs.
Rejoicing in the chase, all-graceful pow'r,
Sweet plant of Venus, Love's delightful flow'r:
Descended from the secret bed divine
Of Pluto's queen, the fair-hair'd Proserpine.
'Tis thine to sink in Tartarus profound,
And shine again thro' heav'ns illustrious round;
Come, timely pow'r, with providential care,
And to thy mystics earth's productions bear [94].

[93] Proclus, in his very elegant hymn to the Sun, celebrates him as frequently called Adonis; and this perfectly agrees with what is said in this and the preceding verse, and with many other parts of the hymn.

[94] " Adonis (says Hermeas, in his Scholia on the Phædrus

LVII.

TO THE TERRESTRIAL HERMES.

THE FUMIGATION FROM STORAX.

HERMES, I call, whom Fate decrees to dwell
Near to Cocytos, the fam'd stream of hell,
And in Necessity's dread path, whose bourn
To none that reach it e'er permits return.
O Bacchic Hermes, progeny divine
Of Dionysius, parent of the vine,
And of celestial Venus, Paphian queen,
Dark-eyelash'd Goddess, of a lovely mien:
Who constant wand'rest thro' the sacred seats
Where Hell's dread empress, Proserpine, retreats:
To wretched souls the leader of the way,
When Fate decrees, to regions void of day.
Thine is the wand which causes sleep to fly,
Or lulls to slumb'rous rest the weary eye;
For Proserpine, thro' Tart'rus dark and wide,
Gave thee for ever flowing souls to guide.
Come, blessed pow'r, the sacrifice attend,
And grant thy mystics' works a happy end.

---

of Plato) presides over every thing that grows and perishes in the earth." επειδη των εν γη φυομενων και αποβιωσκομενων ο δεσποτης Αδωνις εφεστησι. p. 202.

LVIII.

TO LOVE[95].

THE FUMIGATION FROM AROMATICS.

I CALL, great Love, the source of sweet delight,
Holy and pure, and charming to the sight;
Darting, and wing'd, impetuous fierce desire,
With Gods and mortals playing, wand'ring fire:

---

[95] The following development of the nature of the Divinity Love is extracted from the admirable Commentary of Proclus on the First Alcibiades of Plato, as illustrative of the Orphic dogmas respecting this God. " Love is neither to be placed in the first nor among the last of beings. Not in the first, because the object of Love is superior to Love; nor yet among the last, because the lover participates of Love. It is requisite, therefore, that Love should be established between the object of love and the lover, and that it should be posterior to the beautiful, but prior to every nature endued with love. Where then does it first subsist? How does it extend itself through the universe, and with what monads does it leap forth?

" There are three hypostases among the intelligible and occult Gods; and the first, indeed, is characterized by *the good*, understanding *the good itself*, and residing in that place where, according to the [Chaldean] Oracle, the paternal monad abides; but the second is characterized by *wisdom*, where the first intelligence flourishes; and the third by *the beautiful*, where, as Timæus says, the most beautiful of intelligibles abides. But there are three monads according

Agile and twofold, keeper of the keys
Of heav'n and earth, the air, and spreading seas;

to these intelligible causes, subsisting uniformly according to cause in intelligibles, but first unfolding themselves into light in the ineffable order of the Gods, [i. e. in the summit of that order which is called intelligible, and at the same time intellectual,] I mean *faith*, *truth*, and *love*. And faith, indeed, establishes all things in good; but *truth* unfolds all the knowledge in beings; and lastly, *love* converts all things, and congregates them into the nature of the beautiful. This triad thence proceeds through all the orders of the Gods, and imparts to all things by its light a union with the intelligible itself. It also unfolds itself differently in different orders, every where combining its powers with the peculiarities of the Gods. And among some it subsists ineffably, incomprehensibly, and with transcendent union; but among others, as the cause of connecting and binding; and among others, as endued with a perfective and forming power. Here again, it subsists intellectually and paternally; there, in a manner entirely motive, vivific, and effective: here, as governing and assimilating; there, in a liberated and undefiled manner; and elsewhere, according to a multiplied and divided mode. Love, therefore, supernally descends from intelligibles to mundane concerns, calling all things upwards to divine beauty. Truth, also, proceeds through all things, illuminating all things with knowledge. And lastly, faith proceeds through the universe, establishing all things with transcendent union in good. Hence the [Chaldean] Oracles assert, 'that all things are governed by and abide in these.' And, on this account, they order Theurgists to conjoin themselves to divinity through this triad. Intelligibles themselves, indeed, do not require the amatory medium, on account of their ineffable union. But where there is a union and separation of beings, there also Love abides. For it is the binder and conciliator of natures posterior and prior to itself; but the converter of subsequent to

Of all that Ceres' fertile realms contains,
By which th' all parent Goddess life sustains,

prior, and the elevating and perfecting cause of imperfect natures.

"The [Chaldean] Oracles, therefore, speak of Love as binding, and residing in all things; and hence, if it connects all things, it also copulates us with the governments of dæmons. But Diotima calls Love a *great dæmon*, because it every where fills up the medium between desiring and desirable natures. And, indeed, that which is the object of Love vindicates to itself the first order; but that which loves is in the third order from the beloved object. Lastly, Love usurps a middle situation between each, congregating and collecting together that which desires and that which is desired, and filling subordinate from superior natures. But among the intelligible and occult Gods, it unites intelligible intellect to the first and secret beauty, by a certain life better than intelligence. Hence [Orpheus] the theologist of the Greeks calls this Love *blind;* for he says of intelligible intellect,

Ποιμαινων πραπιδεσσιν ανομματον ωκυν ερωτα.

i. e. In his breast feeding *eyeless* rapid Love.

But in natures posterior to intelligibles, it imparts by illumination an indissoluble bond to all things perfected by itself: for a bond is a certain union, but accompanied by much separation. On this account the [Chaldean] Oracles are accustomed to call the fire of this Love *a copulator:* for proceeding from intelligible intellect, it binds all following natures with each other, and with itself. Hence it conjoins all the Gods with intelligible beauty, and dæmons with Gods; but it conjoins us with both Gods and dæmons. In the Gods, indeed, it has a primary subsistence; in dæmons a secondary one; and in partial souls a subsistence through a certain third procession from principles. Again, in the Gods

Or dismal Tartarus is doom'd to keep,
Widely extended, or the sounding deep;
For thee all Nature's various realms obey,
Who rul'st alone, with universal sway.
Come, blessed pow'r, *regard these mystic fires,*
And far avert unlawful mad desires.

it subsists above essence: for every genus of Gods is super-essential. But in dæmons it subsists according to essence: and in souls according to illumination. And this triple order appears similar to the triple power of intellect. For one intellect subsists as imparticipable, being exempt from all partial genera; but another as participated, of which also the souls of the Gods participate as of a better nature; and another is from this ingenerated in souls, and which is, indeed, their perfection." See more concerning this Divinity in the notes on the speech of Diotima in the Banquet of Plato. (Vol. iv. of my Plato.)

LIX.

TO THE FATES.

THE FUMIGATION FROM AROMATICS.

DAUGHTERS of darkling Night, much nam'd, draw near,
Infinite Fates, and listen to my pray'r;
Who in the heavenly lake [96] (where waters white
Burst from a fountain hid in depths of night,
And thro' a dark and stony cavern glide,
A cave profound, invisible) abide;

---

[96] Gesner confesses he is ignorant what the poet means by the λιμνη ουρανια, or *heavenly lake;* as likewise of the *dark cavern* in which Orpheus places the Fates. At first sight, indeed, the whole seems impenetrably obscure; but on comparing this hymn with the sixty-ninth, which is to the Furies, we shall find that the poet expressly calls them the Fates; and places them in an obscure cavern by the holy water of Styx. And from hence it appears, that *the heavenly lake* is the same with *the Stygian pool;* which is called *heavenly,* perhaps because the Gods swear by it. But it is not wonderful that the water is called white; since Hesiod, in Theog. v. 791, speaks of the Stygian waters as falling into the sea with *silvery* whirls. And what strengthens the illustration still more, Fulgentius asserts that the Fates dwell with Pluto.

From whence, wide coursing round the boundless earth,
Your pow'r extends to those of mortal birth;
To men with hope elated, trifling, gay,
A race presumptuous, born but to decay.
To these acceding, in a purple veil
To sense impervious, you yourselves conceal,
When in the plain of Fate you joyful ride
In one great car, with Glory for your guide;
Till all-complete your heav'n-appointed round,
At Justice, Hope, and Care's concluding bound,
The terms absolv'd, prescrib'd by ancient law,
Of pow'r immense, and just without a flaw.
For Fate alone with vision unconfin'd
Surveys the conduct of the mortal kind.
Fate is Jove's perfect and eternal eye,
For Jove and Fate our ev'ry deed descry.
Come, gentle pow'rs, well born, benignant, fam'd,
Atropos, Lachesis, and Clotho nam'd;
Unchang'd, aerial, wand'ring in the night,
Untam'd, invisible to mortal sight;
Fates all-producing, all-destroying, hear,
Regard the incense and the holy pray'r;
Propitious listen to these rites inclin'd,
And far avert distress, with placid mind.

LX.

TO THE GRACES[97].

THE FUMIGATION FROM STORAX.

HEAR me, illustrious Graces, mighty nam'd,
From Jove descended, and Eunomia fam'd,
Thalia and Aglaia fair and bright,
And blest Euphrosyne, whom joys delight:
Mothers of mirth; all lovely to the view,
Pleasure abundant, pure, belongs to you:
Various, for ever flourishing and fair,
Desir'd by mortals, much invok'd in pray'r;
Circling, dark-ey'd, delightful to mankind,
Come, and your mystics' bless with bounteous mind.

[97] In the same manner as Bacchus subsists in Jupiter, and Esculapius in Apollo, so the Graces subsist in Venus, as we are informed by the philosopher Sallust, in his golden Treatise on the Gods and the World.

LXI.

TO NEMESIS.

A HYMN.

THEE, Nemesis, I call, almighty queen,
By whom the deeds of mortal life are seen:
Eternal, much rever'd, of boundless sight,
Alone rejoicing in the just and right:
Changing the counsels of the human breast
For ever various, rolling without rest.
To ev'ry mortal is thy influence known,
And men beneath thy righteous bondage groan;
For ev'ry thought within the mind conceal'd
Is to thy sight perspicuously reveal'd.
The soul unwilling reason to obey,
By lawless passion rul'd, thine eyes survey.
All to see, hear, and rule, O pow'r divine,
Whose nature equity contains, is thine.
Come, blessed, holy Goddess, hear my pray'r,
And make thy mystics' life thy constant care:
Give aid benignant in the needful hour,
And strength abundant to the reas'ning pow'r;
And far avert the dire, unfriendly race
Of counsels impious, arrogant, and base.

LXII.

TO JUSTICE.

THE FUMIGATION FROM FRANKINCENSE.

The piercing eye of Justice bright I sing,
Plac'd by the sacred throne of Jove the king,
Perceiving thence, with vision unconfin'd,
The life and conduct of the human kind [98].
To thee revenge and punishment belong,
Chastising ev'ry deed unjust and wrong.
Whose pow'r alone dissimilars can join,
And from th' equality of truth combine:
For all the ill persuasion can inspire,
When urging bad designs with counsel dire,
'Tis thine alone to punish; with the race
Of lawless passions, and incentives base;
For thou art ever to the good inclin'd,
And hostile to the men of evil mind.
Come, all-propitious, and thy suppliant hear,
Till fates' predestin'd fatal hour draws near.

---

[98] The first four lines of this hymn are, as I have observed in the Introduction, cited by Demosthenes in his first Oration against Aristogiton.

LXIII.

TO EQUITY.

THE FUMIGATION FROM FRANKINCENSE.

O BLESSED Equity, mankind's delight,
Th' eternal friend of conduct just and right:
Abundant, venerable, honour'd maid,
To judgments pure dispensing constant aid,
And conscience stable, and an upright mind;
For men unjust by thee are undermin'd,
Whose souls perverse thy bondage ne'er desire,
But more untam'd decline thy scourges dire.
Harmonious, friendly pow'r, averse to strife,
In peace rejoicing, and a stable life:
Lovely, convivial, of a gentle mind,
Hating excess, to equal deeds inclin'd:
Wisdom and virtue, of whate'er degree,
Receive their proper bound alone in thee.
Hear, Goddess Equity, the deeds destroy
Of evil men, which human life annoy;
That all may yield to thee of mortal birth,
Whether supported by the fruits of earth,
Or in her kindly fertile bosom found,
Or in the realms of marine Jove profound.

LXIV.

TO LAW.

A HYMN.

THE holy king of Gods and men I call,
Celestial Law, the righteous seal of all:
The seal which stamps whate'er the earth contains,
And all conceal'd within the liquid plains:
Stable, and starry, of harmonious frame,
Preserving laws eternally the same.
Thy all-composing pow'r in heav'n appears,
Connects its frame, and props the starry spheres;
And unjust Envy shakes with dreadful sound,
Toss'd by thy arm in giddy whirls around.
'Tis thine the life of mortals to defend,
And crown existence with a blessed end;
For thy command alone, of all that lives,
Order and rule to ev'ry dwelling gives.
Ever observant of the upright mind,
And of just actions the companion kind.
Foe to the lawless, with avenging ire,
Their steps involving in destruction dire.
Come, blest, abundant pow'r, whom all revere,
By all desir'd, with fav'ring mind draw near;
Give me thro' life on thee to fix my sight,
And ne'er forsake the equal paths of right.

LXV.

TO MARS [99].

THE FUMIGATION FROM FRANKINCENSE.

MAGNANIMOUS, unconquer'd, boist'rous Mars,
In darts rejoicing, and in bloody wars;
Fierce and untam'd, whose mighty pow'r can make
The strongest walls from their foundations shake:
Mortal-destroying king, defil'd with gore,
Pleas'd with war's dreadful and tumultuous roar.
Thee human blood [100], and swords, and spears delight,
And the dire ruin of mad savage fight.

---

[99] " Mars, as we are informed by Proclus, in Plat. Repub. p. 388, is the source of division and motion, separating the contrarieties of the universe, which he also perpetually excites, and immutably preserves in order that the world may be perfect and filled with forms of every kind. Hence, also, he presides over war. But he requires the assistance of Venus, that he may insert order and harmony into things contrary and discordant."

[100] " The *slaughter* which is ascribed to Mars (says Hermias, in Plat. Phædr.) signifies a divulsion from matter through rapidly turning from it, and no longer energizing physically, but intellectually. For slaughter, when applied to the Gods, may be said to be an apostacy from secondary natures, just as slaughter in this terrestrial region signifies a privation of the present life."

Stay furious contests, and avenging strife,
Whose works with woe embitter human life;
To lovely Venus and to Bacchus yield,
For arms exchange the labours of the field;
Encourage peace, to gentle works inclin'd,
And give abundance, with benignant mind.

LXVI.

TO VULCAN[101].

THE FUMIGATION FROM FRANKINCENSE AND MANNA.

Strong, mighty Vulcan, bearing splendid light,
Unweary'd fire, with flaming torrents bright:
Strong-handed, deathless, and of art divine,
Pure element, a portion of the world is thine:
All-taming artist, all-diffusive pow'r,
'Tis thine, supreme, all substance to devour:

[101] Vulcan is that divine power which presides over the spermatic and physical productive powers which the universe contains: for whatever Nature accomplishes by verging to bodies, that Vulcan effects in a divine and exempt manner, by moving Nature, and using her as an instrument in his own proper fabrication. For natural heat has a Vulcanian characteristic, and was produced by Vulcan for the purpose of fashioning a corporeal nature. Vulcan, therefore, is that power which perpetually presides over the

Ether, Sun, Moon, and Stars, light pure and clear,
For these thy lucid parts to men appear.
To thee all dwellings, cities, tribes belong,
Diffus'd thro' mortal bodies, rich and strong.
Hear, blessed pow'r, to holy rites incline,
And all propitious on the incense shine:
Suppress the rage of fire's unweary'd frame,
And still preserve our nature's vital flame.

LXVII.

TO ESCULAPIUS [102].

THE FUMIGATION FROM MANNA.

GREAT Esculapius, skill'd to heal mankind,
All-ruling Pæan, and physician kind;
Whose arts medic'nal can alone assuage
Diseases dire, and stop their dreadful rage.

---

fluctuating nature of bodies; and hence, says Olympiodorus, he operates with *bellows*, (εν φυσαις) which occultly signifies his operating in natures (αντι του εν ταις φυσεσι). This deity, also, as well as Mars, as Proclus observes, in Plat. Repub. p. 388, requires the assistance of Venus, in order that he may invest sensible effects with beauty, and thus cause the pulchritude of the world.

[102] This deity, as I have before observed, subsists in Apollo. Proclus, in his very elegant hymn to the Sun, says

Strong, lenient God, regard my suppliant pray'r,
Bring gentle Health, adorn'd with lovely hair;
Convey the means of mitigating pain,
And raging deadly pestilence restrain.
O pow'r all-flourishing, abundant, bright,
Apollo's honour'd offspring, God of light;
Husband of blameless Health, the constant foe
Of dread disease, the minister of woe:
Come, blessed saviour, human health defend[103],
And to the mortal life afford a prosp'rous end.

that Esculapius springs into light from the bland dance of the Sun.

> Σης δ'απο μειλιχοδωρος αλεξικακου θιασειης
> Παιηων βλαστησειν, εην δ'επιτασσειν υγειην,
> Πλησας αρμονιης παναπημονος ευρεα κοσμον.

i. e. " From thy bland dance repelling deadly ill,
Salubrious Pæon blossoms into light,
Health far diffusing, and th' extended world
With streams of harmony innoxious fills."

[103] In the hymn to Apollo, Orpheus, or, as he wrote these hymns for the Mysteries, the initiating priest, *prays for the welfare of all mankind.* Hence, as Esculapius subsists in Apollo, the poet very properly invokes the *healing God* to defend *human* health, or the health of *all men.*

LXVIII.

TO HEALTH.

THE FUMIGATION FROM MANNA.

O MUCH desir'd, prolific, gen'ral queen,
Hear me, life-bearing Health, of beauteous mien,
Mother of all; by thee diseases dire,
Of bliss destructive, from our life retire;
And ev'ry house is flourishing and fair,
If with rejoicing aspect thou art there.
Each dædal art thy vig'rous force inspires,
And all the world thy helping hand desires,
Pluto, life's bane, alone resists thy will,
And ever hates thy all-preserving skill.
O fertile queen, from thee for ever flows
To mortal life from agony repose;
And men without thy all-sustaining ease
Find nothing useful, nothing form'd to please.
Without thy aid, not Pluto's self can thrive,
Nor man to much afflicted age arrive;
For thou alone, of countenance serene,
Dost govern all things, universal queen.
Assist thy mystics with propitious mind,
And far avert disease of ev'ry kind.

LXIX.

TO THE FURIES [104].

THE FUMIGATION FROM AROMATICS.

Vociferous Bacchanalian Furies hear!
Ye I invoke, dread pow'rs, whom all revere;
Nightly, profound, in secret who retire,
Tisiphone, Alecto, and Megara dire:
Deep in a cavern merg'd, involv'd in night,
Near where Styx flows impervious to the sight.
To mankind's impious counsels ever nigh,
Fateful, and fierce to punish these you fly.
Revenge and sorrows dire to you belong,
Hid in a savage vest, severe and strong.

---

[104] See the note on Hymn lix, to the Fates. The Chaldean Oracle observes, " that the Furies are the bonds of men."

Αι ποιναι μεροπων αγκτειραι.

i. e. as Psellus explains it, the powers that punish guilty souls bind them to their material passions, and in these, as it were, suffocate them; such punishment being finally the means of purification. Nor do these powers only afflict the vicious, but even such as convert themselves to an immaterial essence: for these through their connection with matter require a purification of this kind. This illustrates what is said in the seventeenth and three following lines of this hymn.

Terrific virgins, who for ever dwell,
Endu'd with various forms, in deepest hell;
Aerial, and unseen by human kind,
And swiftly coursing, rapid as the mind.
In vain the sun with wing'd effulgence bright [105],
In vain the moon far darting milder light,
Wisdom and virtue may attempt in vain,
And pleasing art, our transport to obtain;
Unless with these you readily conspire,
And far avert your all-destructive ire.
The boundless tribe of mortals you descry,
And justly rule with Right's impartial eye.
Come, snaky-hair'd, Fates many-form'd, divine,
Suppress your rage, and to our rites incline.

---

[105] Ruhnkenius thinks that this and the five following lines should be transferred from hence to the hymn to the Graces; and Hermann adopting this opinion has omitted them in the present hymn, and inserted them in hymn lx. to the Graces. To me, however, it appears that they properly belong to this hymn to the Furies; and therefore I have not transferred them.

LXX.

TO THE FURIES.

THE FUMIGATION FROM AROMATICS.

Hear me, illustrious Furies, mighty nam'd,
Terrific pow'rs, for prudent counsel fam'd;
Holy and pure, from Jove terrestrial born,
And Proserpine, whom lovely locks adorn:
Whose piercing sight with vision unconfin'd
Surveys the deeds of all the impious kind.
On Fate attendant, punishing the race
(With wrath severe) of deeds unjust and base.
Dark-colour'd queens, whose glittering eyes are bright
With dreadful, radiant, life-destroying light:
Eternal rulers, terrible and strong,
To whom revenge and tortures dire belong;
Fateful, and *horrid to the human sight*,
With snaky tresses [106], wand'ring in the night:

---

[106] " Eschylus (says Pausanias, in Attic. cap. 28) was the first that represented the Furies with snakes in their hair." On this passage I have observed in a note in my translation of Pausanias as follows: Those who are of opinion that the Orphic hymns are spurious compositions will doubtless imagine that their opinion is indisputably

Hither approach, and in these rites rejoice,
For ye I call with holy suppliant voice.

confirmed by the present passage: for the Furies, in the
above hymn, are called οφιοπλοκαμοι, or *snaky-haired;* and
consequently, it may be said, they must have been written
posterior to the time of Eschylus, if what Pausanias asserts
be true. It must, however, be remembered, that Eschylus
was accused of inserting in his tragedies things belonging
to the Mysteries; and we have shown, in the Introduction
to these Hymns, that they were used in the Eleusinian
Mysteries. If this be the case, either Pausanias is mistaken in what he asserts of Eschylus in this place; or,
which appears to me to be more probable, being a man
religiously fearful of disclosing any particulars belonging
to the mysteries, he means that no one prior to Eschylus
openly represented the Furies with snakes in their hair.
There is also a passage in the Cataplus of Lucian which
very much corroborates my opinion. The passage is as
follows: ειπε μοι, ετελεσθης γαρ, ω Κυνισκε τα Ελευσινι, ουχ
ομοια τοις εκει τα ενθαδε σοι δοκει; KYN. ευ λεγεις· ιδου ουν
προσερχεται τις δᾳδουχουσα, φοβερον τι, και απειλητικον
προσβλεπουσα· η αρα που Εριννυς εστιν; i. e. Tell me,
Cynic, for your are initiated in the *Eleusinian Mysteries,* do
not the present particulars appear to you to be similar to
those which take place in the Mysteries? Cyn. Very much
so. See then, here comes a certain torch-bearer with *a
dreadful and threatening countenance. Is it, therefore, one of
the Furies?* It is evident from this passage, that the Furies
in the Mysteries were of a terrible appearance, which
Pausanias informs us was not the case with their statues;
and it is from this circumstance of the statues of these
divinities not being dreadful in their appearance, that he
infers Eschylus was the first that represented them to be
so. Hence, as the Mysteries were instituted long before
Eschylus, it is evident that the terrible aspects of the
Furies were not invented by him: and it is more than pro-

LXXI.

TO MELINOE.

THE FUMIGATION FROM AROMATICS.

I CALL, Melinoe, saffron-veil'd, terrene,
Who from dread Pluto's venerable queen,
Mixt with Saturnian Jupiter, arose,
Near where Cocytus' mournful river flows;

bable that this dreadful appearance was principally caused by the snakes in their hair. The present hymn too calls the Furies φοβερωπις, i. e. *terrific to the sight.*

But from what Natales Comes narrates from Menander, it is evident that the snaky tresses of the Furies were not the invention of Eschylus. For he informs us that Menander says, in one of his plays, "it is fabulously reported that Tisiphone became enamoured of a certain beautiful youth, whose name was Cytheron, and that her love for him being very ardent, she contrived the means of conversing with him. He, however, being terrified at her formidable aspect, did not deign to answer her; on which she took one of the *snakes* from her hair and threw it at him, which occasioned his death. But through the commiseration of the Gods, the mountain which was before called Asterius was from him denominated Cytheron." " Fabulati sunt antiqui neque has quidem severissimas Deas Cupidinis vim potuisse devitare, quando scriptum reliquit Mænander in rebus fabulosis, Tisiphonem in amorem cujusdam pueri formosi Cytheronis nomine incidisse, cujus desiderium cum ferre non posset, verba de congressu ad illum proferenda curavit. At is formidandum aspectum veritus, neque responso quidem dig-

When, under Pluto's semblance, Jove divine
Deceiv'd with guileful arts dark Proserpine.
Hence, partly black thy limbs and partly white,
From Pluto dark, from Jove etherial bright.
Thy colour'd members, men by night inspire
When seen in spectred forms, with terrors dire;
Now darkly visible, involv'd in night,
Perspicuous now they meet the fearful sight.
Terrestrial queen, expel wherever found
The soul's mad fears to earth's remotest bound;
With holy aspect on our incense shine,
And bless thy mystics, and the rites divine.

nam fecit, quo illa unum e suis draconibus e capillis convulsum in eum conjecit, quem serpens intra nodos constringens interemit, ubi Deorum misericordia mons ab illo dictus fuit, qui prius Asterius dicebatur." Natalis Comit. Mythol. lib. iii. p. 216. As none of the ancient tragedians, therefore, were the inventors of the fables which are the subjects of their dramas, but derived them from authors more ancient than themselves, it is not at all probable that this fable was invented by Eschylus, and taken by Menander from him,

LXXII.

TO FORTUNE.

THE FUMIGATION FROM FRANKINCENSE.

APPROACH, queen Fortune, with propitious mind
And rich abundance, to my pray'r inclin'd:
Placid and gentle Trivia, mighty nam'd,
Imperial Dian [107], born of Pluto fam'd,

---

[107] Fortune, according to the Platonic, which is the same with the Orphic theology, is that divine power which disposes things differing from each other, and happening contrary to expectation, to beneficent purposes. Or it may be defined to be that divine distribution which causes every thing to fill up the lot assigned to it by the condition of its being. This divinity, too, congregates all sublunary causes, and enables them to confer on sublunary effects that particular good which their nature and merits eminently deserve. "But the power of Fortune (says Simplicius, in Aristot. Physic. lib. ii. p. 81) particularly disposes in an orderly manner the sublunary part of the universe, in which the nature of what is contingent is contained, and which being essentially disordered, Fortune, in conjunction with other primary causes, directs, places in order, and governs. Hence she is represented guiding a rudder, because she governs things sailing on the sea of generation [i. e. of the sublunary world]. Her rudder too is fixed on a globe, because she directs that which is unstable in generation. In her other hand she holds the horn of Amalthea, which is full of fruits, because she is the cause of obtaining all divine fruits. And on this account we venerate the fortunes

Mankind's unconquer'd endless praise is thine,
Sepulch'ral, widely wand'ring pow'r divine!
In thee our various mortal life is found,
And some from thee in copious wealth abound;
While others mourn thy hand averse to bless,
In all the bitterness of deep distress.
Be present, Goddess, to thy vot'ries kind,
And give abundance with benignant mind.

of cities and houses, and of each individual; because being very remote from divine union, we are in danger of being deprived of its participation, and require, in order to obtain it, the assistance of the Goddess Fortune, and of those natures superior to the human, who possess the characteristics of this Divinity. *Indeed, every fortune is good; for every attainment respects something good, nor does any thing evil subsist from divinity. But of things that are good, some are precedaneous, and others are of a punishing or revenging characteristic, which we are accustomed to call evils. Hence we speak of two Fortunes, one of which we denominate* GOOD, *and which is the cause of our obtaining precedaneous good; but the other* EVIL, *which prepares us to receive punishment or revenge.*"

From this beautiful passage, it is easy to see why *Fortune*, in this hymn, is called *Diana*; for each of these divinities governs the sublunary world. See the original of the above admirable extract from Simplicius in the notes to my Pausanias.

LXXIII.

TO THE DÆMON [106].

THE FUMIGATION FROM FRANKINCENSE.

THEE, mighty ruling Dæmon dread, I call,
Mild Jove, life-giving, and the source of all:
Great Jove, much wand'ring, terrible and strong,
To whom revenge and tortures dire belong.
Mankind from thee in plenteous wealth abound,
When in their dwellings joyful thou art found;
Or pass thro' life afflicted and distress'd,
The needful means of bliss by thee suppress'd.
'Tis thine alone, endu'd with boundless might,
To keep the keys of sorrow and delight.
O holy *blessed* father, hear my pray'r,
Disperse the seeds of life-consuming care,
With fav'ring mind the sacred rites attend,
And grant to life a glorious blessed end.

---

[106] According to the Egyptians, as we are informed by Macrobius (in Saturnal. lib. i. cap. 19), the Gods that preside over man at the time of his birth are these four, the *Dæmon, Fortune, Love,* and *Necessity.*" He adds, that by the two former they signified the Sun and Moon; because the Sun, who is the source of spirit, heat, and light, is the generator and guardian of human life; and on this account he is believed to be the dæmon, that is, God of him who is born. But by Fortune they indicated the Moon, because

LXXIV.

TO LEUCOTHEA.

THE FUMIGATION FROM AROMATICS.

I CALL, Leucothea, of great Cadmus born,
And Bacchus' nurse, whom ivy leaves adorn.
Hear, powerful Goddess, in the mighty deep
Vast-bosom'd, destin'd thy domain to keep:
In waves rejoicing, guardian of mankind;
For ships from thee alone deliv'rance find,
Amidst the fury of th' unstable main,
When art no more avails, and strength is vain.
When rushing billows with tempestuous ire
O'erwhelm the mariner in ruin dire,
Thou hear'st with pity touch'd his suppliant pray'r,
Resolv'd his life to succour and to spare.
Be ever present, Goddess! in distress,
Waft ships along with prosp'rous success:
Thy mystics thro' the stormy sea defend,
And safe conduct them to their destin'd end.

---

she presides over bodies which are tossed about through the variety of fortuitous events." Conformably to this, Proclus, in his very elegant hymn to the Sun, invokes that divinity as a *blessed dæmon*,

Αλλα θεων αριστε, πυριστεφες, ολβιε ζαιμων.

LXXV.

TO PALÆMON.

THE FUMIGATION FROM MANNA.

O NURS'D with Dionysius, doom'd to keep
Thy dwelling in the widely spreading deep;
With joyful aspect to my pray'r incline,
Propitious come, and bless the rites divine;
Thy mystics thro' the earth and sea attend,
And from old Ocean's stormy waves defend:
For ships their safety ever owe to thee,
Who wand'rest with them thro' the raging sea.
Come, guardian pow'r, whom mortal tribes desire,
And far avert the deep's destructive ire.

LXXVI.

TO THE MUSES [109].

THE FUMIGATION FROM FRANKINCENSE.

Daughters of Jove, loud-sounding, and divine,
Renown'd, Pierian, sweetly speaking Nine;
To those whose breasts your sacred furies fire,
Much form'd, the objects of supreme desire.
Sources of blameless virtue to mankind,
Who form to excellence the youthful mind:
Who nurse the soul, and give her to descry
The paths of right with reason's steady eye.
Commanding queens, who lead to sacred light
The intellect refin'd from Error's night;
And to mankind each holy rite disclose,
For mystic knowledge from your nature flows.

[109] "The Muses (says Proclus, in Hesiod Op. p. 6) derive their appellation from *investigation:* for they are the sources of erudition. He adds, that Jupiter is said to be the father, and Mnemosyne the mother of the Muses, because the learner ought to possess both intelligence and memory, the latter of which Mnemosyne imparts, and the former Jupiter." See more concerning the Muses in the additional notes.

Clio, and Erato who charms the sight,
With thee, Euterpe, minist'ring delight:
Thalia flourishing, Polymnia fam'd,
Melpomene from skill in music nam'd:
Terpsichore, Urania heav'nly bright,
With thee who gav'st me to behold the light.
Come, venerable, various pow'rs divine,
With fav'ring aspect on your mystics shine;
Bring glorious, ardent, lovely, fam'd desire,
And warm my bosom with your sacred fire.

LXXVII.

TO MNEMOSYNE,

OR THE

Goddess of Memory.

THE FUMIGATION FROM FRANKINCENSE.

THE consort I invoke of Jove divine,
Source of the holy, sweetly speaking Nine;
Free from th' oblivion of the fallen mind,
By whom the soul with intellect is join'd[110].
Reason's increase and thought to thee belong,
All-powerful, pleasant, vigilant, and strong.
'Tis thine to waken from lethargic rest
All thoughts deposited within the breast;
And nought neglecting, vig'rous to excite
The mental eye from dark oblivion's night.
Come, blessed pow'r, thy mystics' mem'ry wake
To holy rites, and Lethe's fetters break.

---

[110] " Memory, says Plotinus, leads to the object of memory." (αγει γαρ η μνημη προς το μνημονευτον.) But the object of memory to the soul is intellect, and the forms or ideas it contains, to which the soul tends through reminiscense; so that the Goddess of Memory is very properly said by Orpheus to conjoin the soul with intellect.

LXXVIII.

TO AURORA.

THE FUMIGATION FROM MANNA.

HEAR me, O Goddess, whose emerging ray
Leads on the broad refulgence of the day;
Blushing Aurora, whose celestial light
Beams on the world with redd'ning splendours bright.
Angel of Titan, whom with constant round
Thy orient beams recall from night profound:
Labour of ev'ry kind to lead is thine,
Of mortal life the minister divine.
Mankind in thee eternally delight,
And none presumes to shun thy beauteous sight.
Soon as thy splendours break the bands of rest,
And eyes unclose, with pleasing sleep oppress'd;
Men, reptiles, birds, and beasts, with gen'ral voice,
And all the nations of the deep rejoice;
For all the culture of our life is thine.
Come, blessed pow'r, and to these rites incline:
Thy holy light increase, and unconfin'd
Diffuse its radiance on thy mystics' mind.

LXXIX.

TO THEMIS.

THE FUMIGATION FROM FRANKINCENSE.

ILLUSTRIOUS Themis, of celestial birth,
Thee I invoke, young blossom of the earth [111].
All-beauteous virgin; first from thee alone
Prophetic oracles to men were known,
Giv'n from the deep recesses of the fane
In sacred Pytho, where renown'd you reign.
From thee Apollo's oracles arose,
And from thy pow'r his inspiration flows.
Honour'd by all, of form divinely bright,
Majestic virgin, wand'ring in the night.
Mankind from thee first learnt perfective rites,
And Bacchus' nightly choirs thy soul delights;
For the God's honours to disclose is thine,
And holy mysteries and rites divine.
Be present, Goddess, to my pray'r inclin'd,
And bless thy Teletæ with fav'ring mind.

---

[111] Themis is one of the progeny of the intellectual Earth resident in Phanes. See the note on Hymn XII, to Hercules.

LXXX.

TO BOREAS[112].

THE FUMIGATION FROM FRANKINCENSE.

Boreas, whose wintry blasts, terrific, tear
The bosom of the deep surrounding air;
Cold icy pow'r, approach, and fav'ring blow,
And Thrace awhile desert, expos'd to snow:
The air's all-misty dark'ning state dissolve,
With pregnant clouds whose frames in show'rs resolve.
Serenely temper all within the sky,
And wipe from moisture Ether's splendid eye.

---

[112] " Orpheus (says Simplicius, in Aristot. de Animâ, lib. i.) appears to have called the aptitude of bodies, with respect to life, *respiration; but the total and universal causes winds,* without which *partial* causes cannot make bodies properly adapted animated."

LXXXI.

TO ZEPHYRUS.

THE FUMIGATION FROM FRANKINCENSE.

Sea-born, aerial, blowing from the west,
Sweet gales, who give to weary'd labour rest.
Vernal and grassy, and of murm'ring sound,
To ships delightful through the sea profound;
For these, impell'd by you with gentle force,
Pursue with prosp'rous fate their destin'd course.
With blameless gales regard my suppliant pray'r,
Zephyrs unseen, light-wing'd, and form'd from air.

LXXXII.

TO THE SOUTH WIND.

THE FUMIGATION FROM FRANKINCENSE.

Wide-coursing gales, whose lightly leaping feet
With rapid wings the air's wet bosom beat,
Approach, benevolent, swift-whirling pow'rs,
With humid clouds the principles of show'rs;
For show'ry clouds are portion'd to your care,
To send on earth from all-surrounding air.
Hear, blessed pow'r, these holy rites attend,
And fruitful rains on earth all-parent send.

LXXXIII.

TO OCEAN[113].

THE FUMIGATION FROM AROMATICS.

Ocean I call, whose nature ever flows,
From whom at first both Gods and men arose;
Sire incorruptible, whose waves surround,
And earth's all-terminating circle bound:

[113] Ocean, as I have before observed in the note on the hymn to Hercules, according to its first subsistence, is one of the offspring of the first intellectual Earth. "And of the divine Titannic hebdomads (says Proclus, in Tim. lib. v. p. 292) Ocean both abides and proceeds, uniting himself to his father [Heaven] and not departing from his kingdom. But all the rest of the Titans, rejoicing in progression, are said to have given completion to the will of Earth, but to have assaulted their father, dividing themselves from his kingdom, and proceeding into another order. Or rather, of all the celestial genera, some alone abide in their principles, as the two first triads." "For (says Orpheus) as soon as Heaven understood that they had an implacable heart and a lawless nature, he hurled them into Tartarus, the profundity of the earth." He concealed them, therefore, in the unapparent, through transcendency of power. But others both abide in and proceed from their principles, as Ocean and Tethys. For when the other Titans proceeded to assault their father Heaven, Ocean prohibited them from obeying the mandates of their mother, being dubious of their rectitude.

"But Ocean (says Orpheus) remained within his place of

Hence every river, hence the spreading sea,
And earth's pure bubbling fountains spring from thee.
Hear, mighty sire, for boundless bliss is thine,
Greatest cathartic of the pow'rs divine:

abode, considering to what he should direct his attention,
and whether he should deprive his father of strength, and
unjustly mutilate him in conjunction with Saturn, and the
other brethren, who were obedient to their dear mother; or
leaving these, stay quietly at home. After much fluctuation
of thought, however, he remained peaceably at home, being
angry with his mother, but still more so with his brethren."
He therefore abides, and at the same time proceeds together
with Tethys; for she is conjoined with him according to
the first progeny. But the other Titans are induced to
separation and progression. And the leader of these is the
mighty Saturn, as the theologist says; though he evinces
that Saturn is superior to Ocean, by saying that Saturn
himself received the celestial Olympus, and that there
being throned, he reigns over the Titans; but that Ocean
obtained all the middle allotment. For he says, " that Ocean
dwells in the divine streams which are posterior to Olympus,
and that he environs the Heaven which is there, and
not the highest Heaven, but as the fable says, that which
fell from Olympus, and was there arranged."

As the latter part of what is here said from Proclus, is a
very remarkable Orphic fragment, and is not to be found in
the Collection of the Orphic remains by either Gesner or
Hermann, I shall give the original for the sake of the
learned reader. Και τοι γε οτι ο Κρονος υπιρτερος εστι του
Οκεανου, δεδηλωκεν ο θεολογος παλιν λεγων· τον μεν Κρονον
ουτον καταλαμβανειν τον ουρανιον Ολυμπον, κᾳκει θρονισ-
θεντα, βασιλευειν των Τιτανων· τον δε Οκεανον την ληξιν
απασαν την μεσην· ναιειν γαρ αυτον εν τοις θεσπεσιοις
ρειθροις τοις μετα τον Ολυμπον, και τον εκει περιεπειν Ουρανον,

Earth's friendly limit, fountain of the pole,
Whose waves wide spreading and circumfluent roll.
Approach benevolent, with placid mind,
And be for ever to thy mystics kind.

αλλ' ου τον ακροτατον, ως δε φησιν ο μυθος, τον εμπεσοντα του Ουλυμπου, και εκει τεταγμενον.

Proclus also, in p. 298, speaking of the nine deities mentioned by Plato in the Timæus, according to their *sublunary* allotment; for they originally proceed from the intellectual order, says: " Heaven terminates, Earth corroborates, and *Ocean* moves all generation. But Tethys establishes every thing in its proper motion; intellectual essences in intellectual, middle essences in physical [or such as pertain to soul], and such as are corporeal in psychical motion; *Ocean* at the same time collectively moving all things. Saturn alone divides intellectually; Rhea vivifies; Phorcys distributes spermatic productive principles; Jupiter perfects things apparent from such as are unapparent; and Juno evolves according to the all-various mutations of visible natures."

LXXXIV.

TO VESTA [114].

THE FUMIGATION FROM AROMATICS.

Daughter of Saturn, venerable dame,
Who dwell'st amidst great fire's eternal flame;

---

[114] " Saturn (says Proclus, in Cratyl, p. 83) in conjunction with Rhea, produced Vesta and Juno, who are coordinate with the demiurgic causes. For Vesta imparts from herself to the Gods an uninclining permanency and seat in themselves, and an indissoluble essence. But Juno imparts progression, and a multiplication into things secondary. She is also the vivifying fountain of wholes, and the mother of prolific powers; and on this account she is said to have proceeded together with Jupiter the Demiurgus; and through this communion she generates maternally such things as Jupiter generates paternally. But Vesta abides in herself, possessing an undefiled virginity, and being the cause of sameness to all things. Each of these divinities, however, together with her own proper perfection, possesses according to participation the power of the other. Hence some say that Vesta is denominated from *essence*, (απο της εσσιας*, lege ουσιας) looking to her proper hyparxis. But others, surveying her vivific and motive power, which she derives from Juno, say that she is thus denominated *as being the cause of impulsion.* (ως ωσεως ουσαν αιτιαν.) For all

---

* My manuscript has ισσιας· but the edition of this work, by the very learned Professor Boissonade, Leipsic, 1820, has εσσιας. The true reading however is doubtless ουσιας.

In sacred rites these ministers are thine,
Mystics much blessed, holy, and divine.

divine natures are in all, and particularly such as are coordinate with each other, participate of, and subsist in each other. Each, therefore, of the demiurgic and vivific orders participates the form by which it is characterized from Vesta. The orbs of the planets, likewise, possess the sameness of their revolutions from her; and the poles and centres are always allotted from her their permanent rest. Vesta, however, does not manifest essence, but the abiding and firm establishment of essence in itself; and hence this Goddess proceeds into light after the mighty Saturn. For the Divinities prior to Saturn have not a subsistence in themselves and in another, but this originates from Saturn. And a subsistence in *self* is the peculiarity of Vesta, but in *another* of Juno." What is here said by Proclus about a subsistence in *self* and in *another*, the reader will find explained in the notes on my translation of the Parmenides of Plato.

In addition to the above admirable development of the nature of Vesta by Proclus, it is necessary to add, that this Goddess, according to her mundane allotment, is the Divinity of the Earth; and as such she is celebrated in the present hymn. Hence Philolaus, in a fragment preserved by Stobæus (Eclog. Phys. p. 51), says, "that there is a fire in the middle at the centre, which is the Vesta of the universe, the house of Jupiter, the mother of the Gods, and the basis, coherence, and measure of nature." Hence it appears that they are greatly mistaken who suppose the Pythagoreans meant the Sun by the fire at the centre; and this is still more evident from what Simplicius says in his Commentary on Arist. de Cœlo, lib. ii. for he there observes, "that the Pythagoreans supposing the decad to be a perfect number, were willing to collect the bodies that are moved in a circle into the decadic number. Hence they say, that the inerratic sphere, the seven planets, this our earth, and

In thee the Gods have fix'd their dwelling place,
Strong, stable basis of the mortal race.

the antichthon complete the decad; and in this manner Aristotle understands the assertions of the Pythagoreans." He then adds: Οι δε γνησιεστερον αυτων μετασχοντες, το μεν πυρ εν τῳ μεσῳ φασι την δημιουργικην δυναμιν, εκ του μεσου ολην την γην τρεφουσαν, και το ψυχομενον αυτης ανεγειρουσαν· δι ο, οι μεν Ζηνος πυργον αυτο καλουσιν, ως αυτος εν τοις Πυθαγορειοις διηγησατο· οι δέ Διος φυλακην, ως εν τουτοις· οι δε Διος θρονον· ως αλλοι φασιν· αντρον δε την γην ελεγον, ως οργανον και αυτην του χρονου· ημερων γαρ εστιν αυτη, και νυκτων, αιτια. i. e. "But those who more genuinely participate of the Pythagorean doctrines say that the fire in the middle is a demiurgic power, nourishing the whole earth from the middle, and exciting whatever it contains of a frigid nature. Hence some call it the tower of Jupiter, as he (i. e. Aristotle) narrates in his Pythagorics. But others denominate it the guardian of Jupiter, as Aristotle relates in the present treatise. And according to others it is the throne of Jupiter. They called, however, the earth a cavern, as being itself an instrument of time: for it is the cause of day and night." In that part of this remarkable passage, in which it is said that the Pythagoreans called the earth *a cavern*, it is necessary for αντρον to read αστρον, *a star*. For a little before both Aristotle and Simplicius inform us, that the Pythagoreans asserted that *the earth exists as one of the stars*. And this is confirmed by their calling the earth one of the *instruments of time:* for the stars are thus denominated by Plato in the Timæus. Meursius, in his Denarius Pythagoricus, p. 19, thinks we should read κεντρον for αντρον; but he was evidently mistaken.

From this account, given by Simplicius, it appears that the abovementioned decad of the Pythagoreans consists of the inerratic sphere, the seven planets, the earth, and the fire in the centre of the earth.

Eternal, much form'd, ever florid queen,
Laughing [115] and blessed, and of lovely mien;
Accept these rites, accord each just desire,
And gentle health and needful good inspire.

[115] "The *laughter* of the Gods (says Proclus, in Plat. Polit. p. 384) must be defined to be their exuberant energy in the universe, and the cause of the gladness of all mundane natures. But as such a providence is incomprehensible, and the communication of all good from the Gods is never failing, Homer very properly calls their laughter unextinguished." He adds, "fables, however, do not assert that the Gods always weep, but that they laugh without ceasing. For tears are symbols of their providence in mortal and frail concerns, and which now rise into existence, and then perish; but laughter is a sign of their energy in wholes, and those perfect natures in the universe which are perpetually moved with undeviating sameness. On which account, I think, when we divide demiurgic productions into Gods and men, we attribute laughter to the generation of the Gods, but tears to the formation of men and animals; whence a certain poet, in his hymn to the Sun, says

> Mankind's laborious race thy tears excite,
> But the Gods, *laughing*, blossom'd into light.

But when we make a division into things celestial and sublunary, again, after the same manner, we must assign *laughter* to the former and tears to the latter. And when we reason concerning the generations and corruptions of sublunary natures themselves, we must refer the former to the *laughter*, and the latter to the *tears* of the Gods. Hence in the mysteries also, those who preside over sacred institutions order both these to be celebrated at stated times."

LXXXV.

TO SLEEP.

THE FUMIGATION FROM A POPPY.

Sleep, king of Gods, and men of mortal birth,
Sov'reign of all, sustain'd by mother Earth;
For thy dominion is supreme alone,
O'er all extended, and by all things known.
'Tis thine all bodies with benignant mind
In other bands than those of brass to bind.
Tamer of cares, to weary toil repose,
And from whom sacred solace in affliction flows.
Thy pleasing gentle chains preserve the soul,
And e'en the dreadful cares of death control;
For Death, and Lethe with oblivious stream,
Mankind thy genuine brothers justly deem.
With fav'ring aspect to my pray'r incline,
And save thy mystics in their works divine.

LXXXVI.

TO THE DIVINITY OF DREAMS.

THE FUMIGATION FROM AROMATICS.

Thee I invoke, blest pow'r of dreams divine,
Angel of future fates, swift wings are thine.
Great source of oracles to human kind,
When stealing soft, and whisp'ring to the mind,
Thro' sleep's sweet silence, and the gloom of night,
Thy pow'r awakes th' intellectual sight;
To silent souls the will of heaven relates,
And silently reveals their future fates.
Forever friendly to the upright mind,
Sacred and pure, to holy rites inclin'd;
For these with pleasing hope thy dreams inspire:
Bliss to anticipate, which all desire.
Thy visions manifest of fate disclose,
What methods best may mitigate our woes;
Reveal what rites the Gods immortal please,
And what the means their anger to appease;
For ever tranquil is the good man's end,
Whose life thy dreams admonish and defend.

But from the wicked turn'd averse to bless,
Thy form unseen, the angel of distress;
No means to check approaching ill they find,
Pensive with fears, and to the future blind.
Come, blessed pow'r, the signatures reveal
Which heav'n's decrees mysteriously conceal,
Signs only present to the worthy mind,
Nor omens ill disclose of monstrous kind.

LXXXVII.

TO DEATH [116].

THE FUMIGATION FROM MANNA.

Hear me, O Death, whose empire unconfin'd
Extends to mortal tribes of ev'ry kind.
On thee the portion of our time depends,
Whose absence lengthens life, whose presence ends.

---

[116] Hermann's edition of these Orphic *Teletai* ends with a hymn to Mars, which is found among the hymns ascribed to Homer; both he and Ruhnkenius being of opinion that it is more Orphic than Homeric. I, however, should say, that it was written by any one rather than by Orpheus.

Thy sleep perpetual bursts the vivid folds
By which the soul attracting body holds [117]:

For can it for a moment be supposed that Orpheus would pray that he might be able

Θυμου τ'αυ μενος οξυ κατισχεμεν, ος μ'ερεθησι
Φυλοπιδος κρυερης επιβαινεμεν.——

"To restrain the impetuous force of anger, which excites him to engage in horrid war!"

[117] What is said in this and the preceding line is well explained by Porphyry in his excellent treatise entitled Αφορμαι προς τα νοητα, or *Auxiliaries to the Perception of Intelligibles*, viz. "That which nature binds, nature also dissolves: and that which the soul binds, the soul likewise dissolves. Nature, indeed, bound the body to the soul; but the soul binds herself to the body. Nature, therefore, liberates the body from the soul; but the soul liberates herself from the body." And again, in the next sentence, "Hence there is a twofold death; the one, indeed, universally known, in which the body is liberated from the soul; but the other peculiar to philosophers, in which the soul is liberated from the body. Nor does the one entirely follow the other." The meaning of this twofold death is as follows: Though the body, by the death which is universally known, may be loosened from the soul, yet while material passions and affections reside in the soul, the soul will continually verge to another body, and as long as this inclination continues, remain connected with body. But when, from the predominance of an intellectual nature, the soul is separated from material affections, it is truly liberated from the body; though the body at the same time verges and clings to the soul, as to the immediate cause of its support.

Common to all, of ev'ry sex and age,
For nought escapes thy all-destructive rage.
Not youth itself thy clemency can gain,
Vig'rous and strong, by thee untimely slain.
In thee the end of nature's works is known,
In thee all judgment is absolv'd alone.
No suppliant arts thy dreadful rage control,
No vows revoke the purpose of thy soul.
O blessed pow'r, regard my ardent pray'r,
And human life to age abundant spare.

ADDITIONAL NOTES.

THE following Additional Notes are given for the purpose of elucidating the Orphic theology, with which the preceding hymns are replete. They form the greater part of the Scholia of Proclus on the Cratylus of Plato, a work inestimably valuable to the student of the Grecian theology, and which has been recently published with very valuable critical notes by the most learned Professor Boissonade. The following translation, however, was made by me many years ago from a manuscript of this work, which is a copy of an original in the possession of Mr. Heber, and which is so very rare that it is not to be found either in the Bodleian Library or the British Museum, nor, I believe, in any of the public libraries of Great Britain. I have given the translation of these Scholia in the order in which they occur in the original, as I could not have done otherwise without omitting some part of them, which, on account of their great importance, I was unwilling to do.

JUPITER is not *said to be*, but *is*, the father of those who genuinely preserve the proper form of life, such as Hercules and the Dioscuri; but of those who are never at any time able to convert themselves to a divine nature, he never *is* nor is *said to be* the father. Such therefore, as having been partakers of a certain energy above human nature, have again fallen into *the sea of dissimilitude*[1], and for honour among men have embraced error towards the Gods, —of these Jupiter is *said to be* the father.

The paternal cause originates supernally from the intelligible and occult Gods; for there the first fathers of wholes subsist; but it proceeds through all the intellectual Gods into the demiurgic order. For Timæus celebrates this order as at the same time *fabricative* and *paternal;* since he calls Jupiter the *demiurgus* and *father*. The fathers, however, who are superior to the one fabrication are called Gods of Gods, but the demiurgus is the father of Gods and men. Farther still, Jupiter is said to be *peculiarly* the father of some, as of Hercules, who immutably preserve a Jovian and ruling life during their converse with the realms of generation. Jupiter, therefore, is triply father, of gods, partial souls, and of souls that embrace an intellectual and Jovian life. The intellectual order of the gods, therefore, is supernally bounded by the king[2] of the total divine genera, and who has a paternal transcendency with respect to all the intellectual Gods. This king, according to Orpheus, is called by the blessed immortals that dwell on lofty Olympus, Phanes Protogonus. But this order proceeds through the three Nights, and the celestial orders, into the Titanic or Saturnian series, where it first separates itself from the fathers, and changes the kingdom of the *Synoches*[3] for a distributive government of wholes, and unfolds every demiurgic genus of the Gods from all the abovementioned ruling and royal causes, but proximately from Saturn, the leader of the Titanic orders. Prior, however, to other fabricators ($δημιουργοι$) it unfolds Jupiter, who is allotted the unical strength of the whole demiurgic

[1] Plato, in the Politicus, thus calls the realms of generation, i. e. the whole of a visible nature.

[2] That is, intelligible intellect, the extremity of the intelligible order.

[3] That is, the divinities who compose the middle of that order of Gods which is denominated intelligible and at the same time intellectual.

series, and who produces and gives subsistence to all unapparent and apparent natures. And he is indeed intellectual, according to the order in which he ranks, but he produces the species and the genera of beings into the order of sensibles. He is likewise filled with the Gods above himself, but imparts from himself a progression into being to all mundane natures. Hence Orpheus [4] represents him fabricating every celestial race, making the sun and moon and the other starry Gods, together with the sublunary elements, and diversifying the latter with forms which before had a disordered subsistence. He likewise represents him presiding over the Gods who are distributed about the whole world, and who are suspended from him; and in the character of a legislator assigning distributions of providence in the universe according to desert to all the mundane Gods. Homer too, following Orpheus, celebrates him as the common father of Gods and men, as leader and king, and as the supreme of rulers. He also says that all the multitude of mundane Gods is collected about him, abides in and is perfected by him. For all the mundane Gods are converted to Jupiter through Themis,

ζευς δε θεμιστα κελευσε θεους, αγορην δε καλεσσαι.
―――――――― ηδ, αρα παντη
φοιτησασα κελευσε Διος προς δωμα νεεσθαι.

i. e. "But Jupiter orders Themis to call the Gods to council; and she directing her course every where commands them to go to the house of Jupiter [5]." All of them therefore are excited according to the one will of Jupiter, and

---

[4] As what is here said from Orpheus concerning Jupiter is very remarkable, and is no where else to be found, I give the original for the sake of the learned reader. διο και Ορφευς δημιουργουντα μεν αυτον την ουρανιαν πασαν γενεαν παραδιδωσι, και ηλιον ποιουντα και σεληνην, και τους αλλους αστρους θεους· δημιουργουντα δε τα υποσεληνη στοιχεια, και διακρινοντα τοις ειδεσιν ατακτως εχοντα προτερον· στεφας δ' εφιστωντα θεων περι ολον τον κοσμον εις αυτον ανηρτημενας, και διαθεσμοθετουντα πασι τοις εγκοσμιοις θεοις κατ' αξιαν διανομας της εν τω παντι προνοιας.

[5] Iliad, xx. 4.

become διος ενδον[6], *within Jupiter*, as the poet says. Jupiter too again separates them within himself, according to two coordinations, and excites them to providential energies about secondary natures; he at the same time, as Timæus says, abiding after his accustomed manner;

ως εφατο κρονιδης πολεμον δ' αλιαστον εγειρεν[7].

i. e. " Thus spoke Saturnian Jupiter, and excited inevitable war." Jupiter however is separate and exempt from all mundane natures; whence also the most total and leading of the other Gods, though they appear to have in a certain respect equal authority with Jupiter, through a progression from the same causes, yet call him father. For both Neptune and Juno celebrate him by this appellation. And though Juno speaks to him as one who is of the same order,

και γαρ εγο θεος ειμι· γενος δε μοι ενθεν οθεν σοι,
και με πρεσβυτατην τεκετο κρονος αγκυλομητις[8].

i. e. " For I also am a divinity, and Saturn, of inflected counsel, endowed me with the greatest dignity, when he begot me."

And though Neptune says,

τρεις' γαρ τ'εκ κρονου ειμεν αδελφεοι, ους τεκε Ρειη,
Ζευς και εγω, τριτατος δ'Αἰδης ενεροισιν ανασσων[9].

i. e. " For we are three brothers from Saturn, whom Rhea bore, Jupiter and I, and the third is Pluto, who governs the infernal realms :"

Yet Jupiter is called father by both these divinities; and this because he comprehends in himself the one and impartible cause of all fabrication; is prior to the Saturnian

[6] See the 14th line. [7] Ibid, 32.
[8] Iliad, iv. 58. [9] Iliad, xv. 187.

ADDITIONAL NOTES. 169

triad[10]; connectedly contains the three fathers; and comprehends on all sides the vivification of Juno. Hence, at the same time that this goddess gives animation to the universe, he also, together with other Gods, gives subsistence to souls. Very properly therefore do we say that the demiurgus in the Timæus is the mighty Jupiter. For he it is who produces mundane intellects and souls, who adorns all bodies with figures and numbers, and inserts in them one union, and an indissoluble friendship and bond. For Night also, in Orpheus, advises Jupiter to employ things of this kind in the fabrication of the universe.

αυταρ επην δεσμον κρατερον περι πασι ταννασης.

i. e. But when your power around the whole has spread
A strong coercive bond.—

The proximate bond indeed of mundane natures is that which subsists through analogy; but the more perfect bond is derived from intellect and soul. Hence Timæus calls the communion of the elements through analogy, and the indissoluble union from life, a bond. For he says, animals were generated bound with animated bonds. But a more venerable bond than these subsists from the demiurgic will. " For my will, says Jupiter in the Timæus, is a greater and more principal bond, &c."

Firmly adhering therefore to this conception respecting the mighty Jupiter, viz. that he is the demiurgus and father of the universe, that he is an all-perfect imparticipable[11] intellect, and that he fills all things both with other goods, and with life, let us survey how from names Socrates unfolds the mystic truth concerning this divinity. Timæus then says that it is difficult to know the essence of the

---

[10] For the Saturnian triad belongs to that order of Gods which is called supermundane, and which immediately subsists after the intellectual order; so that the Jupiter who ranks at the summit of this triad is different from and inferior to the demiurgus.

[11] That is, he is not an intellect consubsistent with soul.

demiurgus, and Socrates now says that it is not easy to understand his name, which manifests his power and energy.

Again, our soul knows partibly the impartible nature of the energy of the Gods, and that which is characterized by unity in this energy, in a multiplied manner: and this especially takes place about the demiurgus who expands intellectual forms, and calls forth intelligible causes, and evolves them to the fabrication of the universe. For Parmenides characterizes him by sameness and difference. According to Homer, two tubs are placed near him; and the most mystic tradition and the oracles of the Gods say that the duad is seated with him. For thus they speak: " He possesses both; containing intelligibles in intellect, but introducing sense to the worlds." These oracles likewise call him *twice beyond*, and *twice there* (διç επεκεινα και διç εκει). And, in short, they celebrate him through the duad. For the demiurgus comprehends in himself unitedly every thing *prolific*[12], and which gives subsistence to mundane natures. Very properly therefore is his name two fold, of which δια manifests *the cause through which,* and this is paternal goodness; but ζηνα signifies *vivification,* the first causes of which in the universe the demiurgus unically comprehends. The former too is a symbol of the Saturnian and paternal series; but the latter of the vivific and maternal Rhea. So far likewise as Jupiter receives the whole of Saturn, he gives subsistence to a triple essence, the impartible, the partible, and that which subsists between these; but according to the Rhea which he contains in himself, he scatters as from a fountain, intellectual, psychical, and corporeal life. But by his demiurgic powers and energies, he gives a formal subsistence to these, and separates them from forms of a prior order, and from each other. He is also the ruler and king of all things: and is exempt from the three demiurgi. For they, as Socrates says in the

---

[12] And the duad, considered as a divine form or idea, is the source of fecundity.

ADDITIONAL NOTES.

Gorgias, divide the kingdom of their father; but Jupiter the demiurgus at once, without division, reigns over the three, and unically governs them.

He is therefore the cause of the paternal triad, and of all fabrication; but he connectedly contains the three demiurgi. And he is a *king* indeed, as being coordinated with the fathers; but a *ruler*, as being proximately established above the demiurgic triad, and comprehending the uniform cause of it. Plato therefore, by considering his name in two ways, evinces that images receive partibly the unical causes of paradigms, and that this is adapted to him who establishes the intellectual duad in himself. For he gives subsistence to twofold orders, the celestial and the supercelestial; whence also the theologist Orpheus says, that his sceptre consists of four and twenty measures, as ruling over a twofold twelve [13].

Farther still, the soul of the world gives life to altermotive natures; for to these it becomes the fountain and principle of motion, as Plato says in the Phædrus and Laws. But the demiurgus simply imparts to all things life divine, intellectual, psychical, and that which is divisible about bodies. No one however should think that the Gods in their generations of secondary natures are diminished; or that they sustain a division of their proper essence in giving subsistence to things subordinate; or that they expose their progeny to the view, externally to themselves, in the same manner as the causes of mortal offspring. Nor in short, must we suppose that they generate with motion or mutation, but that abiding in themselves, they produce by their very essence posterior natures, comprehend on all sides their progeny, and supernally perfect the productions and

---

[13] i. e. The twelve Gods who first subsist in the *liberated* or supercelestial order, and who are divided into four triads, and the twelve mundane Gods, Jupiter, Neptune, Vulcan; Vesta, Minerva, Mars; Ceres, Juno, Diana; and Mercury, Venus, Apollo. The first of these triads is *fabricative;* the second *defensive;* the third *vivific;* and the fourth *anagogic* or *elevating*, as is shown by Proclus in the sixth book of his Theology.

energies of their offspring. Nor again, when it is said that Gods are the sons of more total Gods, must it be supposed that they are disjoined from more ancient causes, and are cut off from a union with them: or that they receive the peculiarity of their hyparxis through motion, and an indefiniteness converting itself to bound. For there is nothing irrational and without measure in the natures superior to us. But we must conceive that their progressions are effected through similitude; and that there is one communion of essence, and an indivisible continuity of powers and energies, between the sons of Gods and their fathers; all those Gods that rank in the second order being established in such as are more ancient; and the more ancient imparting much of perfection, vigour, and efficacious production to the subordinate. And after this manner we must understand that Jupiter is said to be the son of Saturn. For Jupiter, being the demiurgic intellect, proceeds from another intellect, superior and more uniform, which increases indeed its proper intellections, but converts the multitude of them to union; and multiplies its intellectual powers, but elevates their all-various evolutions to impartible sameness. Jupiter therefore proximately establishing a communion with this divinity, and being filled from him with total intellectual good, is very properly said to be the son of Saturn, both in hymns and in invocations, as unfolding into light that which is occult, expanding that which is contracted, and dividing that which is impartible in the Saturnian monad; and as emitting a second more partial kingdom, instead of that which is more total, a demiurgic instead of a paternal dominion, and an empire which proceeds every where instead of that which stably abides in itself.

Why does Socrates apprehend the name of king Saturn to be *υβριστικον*, *insolent*, and looking to what does he assert this? We reply, that according to the poets *satiety* (*κορος*) is the cause of *insolence;* for they thus denominate immoderation and repletion; and they say that *Satiety* brought forth *Insolence* (*υβριν φασιν τικτει κορος*). He there-

ADDITIONAL NOTES. 173

fore who looks without attention to the name of Saturn will consider it as signifying *insolence*. For to him who suddenly hears it, it manifests satiety and repletion. Why therefore, since a name of this kind is expressive of insolence, do we not pass it over in silence, as not being auspicious and adapted to the Gods? May we not say that the royal series [14] of the Gods, beginning from Phanes and ending in Bacchus, and producing the same sceptre supernally as far as to the last kingdom, Saturn being allotted the fourth royal order, appears according to the fabulous pretext, differently from the other kings, to have received the sceptre insolently from Heaven, and to have given it to Jupiter? For Night receives the sceptre from Phanes;

---

[14] This royal series consists of Phanes, Night, Heaven, Saturn, Jupiter, Bacchus. "Ancient theologists (says Syrianus, in his Commentary on the fourteenth book of Aristotle's Metaphysics) assert that Night and Heaven reigned, and prior to these the mighty father of Night and Heaven, who distributed the world to Gods and mortals, and who first possessed royal authority, the illustrious Ericapæus.

τοισι μεν διενειμε θεοις, θνητοισι δε κοσμον
ου πρωτος βασιλευε περικλυτος ηρικεπαιος.

Night succeeded Ericapæus, in the hands of whom she has a sceptre:

σκηπτρον εχους' εν χερσιν ηρικεπαιου.

To Night Heaven succeeded, who first reigned over the Gods after mother Night.

ος πρωτος βασιλευε θεων μετα μητερα νυκτα.

Chaos transcends the habitude of sovereign dominion: and, with respect to Jupiter, the oracles given to him by Night manifestly call him not the first, but the fifth immortal king of the Gods.

αθανατον βασιλεα θεων πεμπτον γενεσθαι.

According to these theologists therefore, that principle which is most eminently the first, is *the one* or *the good*, after which, according to Pythagoras, are those two principles Æther and Chaos, which are superior to the possession of sovereign dominion. In the next place succeed the first and occult genera of the Gods, in which first shines forth the father and king of all wholes, and whom on this account they call *Phanes*."

Heaven derives from Night the dominion over wholes; and Bacchus, who is the last king of the Gods, receives the kingdom from Jupiter. For the father (Jupiter) establishes him in the royal throne, puts into his hand the sceptre, and makes him the king of all the mundane Gods. "Hear me, ye Gods, I place over you a king."

κλυτε θεοι τον δ'υμμιν βασιλεα τιθημι.

says Jupiter to the junior Gods. But Saturn alone perfectly deprives Heaven of the kingdom, and concedes dominion to Jupiter, cutting and being cut off, as the fable says. Plato therefore seeing this succession, which in Saturn is called by theologists *insolent* (υβριστικη), thought it worth while to mention the appearance of insolence in the name; that from this he might evince the name is adapted to the God, and that it bears an image of the insolence which is ascribed to him in fables. At the same time he teaches us to refer mythical devices to the truth concerning the Gods, and the apparent absurdity which they contain to scientific conceptions.

The great, when ascribed to the Gods, must not be considered as belonging to interval, but as subsisting intellectually, and according to the power of cause, but not according to partible transcendency. But why does Plato now call Saturn διανοια, the dianoetic part of the soul? May we not say, that it is because he looks to the multitude of intellectual conceptions in him, the orders of intelligibles, and the evolution of forms which he contains; since also in the Timæus, he represents the demiurgic intellect as reasoning, and making the world, dianoetically energizing: and this in consequence of looking to his partible and divided intellections, according to which he fabricates not only wholes, but parts. When Saturn, however, is called-intellect, Jupiter has the order of the dianoetic part: and when again, Saturn is called the dianoetic part, we must say that he is so called according to analogy with reference to a certain other intellect of a higher order. Whether therefore you are willing to speak of intelligible and occult

ADDITIONAL NOTES.   175

intellect, or of that which unfolds into light (εκφαντορικος νους), or of that which connectedly contains (συνεκτικος νους), or of that which imparts perfection[15] (τελεσιουργος νους), Saturn will be as the dianoetic part to all these. For he produces united intellection into multitude, and fills himself wholly with excited intelligibles. Whence also he is said to be the leader of the Titannic race, and the source of all-various separation and diversifying power. And perhaps Plato here primarily delivers twofold interpretations of the name of the Titans, which Iamblicus and Amelius afterwards adopted. For the one interprets this name from the Titans extending their powers to all things; but the other from *something insectile* (παρα το τι ατομον), because the division and separation of wholes into parts receives its beginning from the Titans. Socrates therefore now indicates both these interpretations, by asserting of the king of the Titans that he is a *certain great dianoetic power*. For the term *great* is a symbol of power pervading to all things; but the term *a certain*, of power proceeding to the most partial natures.

The name Saturn is now triply analysed; of which the first asserting this God to be the plenitude of intellectual good, and to be the satiety of a divine intellect, from its conveying an image of the satiety and repletion which are reprobated by the many, is ejected as insolent. The second also, which exhibits the imperfect and the puerile, is in like manner rejected. But the third, which celebrates this God as full of purity, and as the leader of undefiled intelligence, and an undeviating life, is approved. For king Saturn is intellect, and the supplier of all intellectual life; but he is an intelligible exempt from coordination with sensibles, immaterial and separate, and converted to himself. He likewise converts his progeny, and after producing them

---

[15] Of these intellects the first is Phanes, the second Heaven, the third Earth, and the fourth the Subcelestial Arch, which is celebrated in the Phædrus, viz. νους νοητος ο φανης; εκφαντορικος νους ο Ουρανος, συνεκτικος νους η γη, τελεσιουργος δε νους η υπ'ουρανιος αψις.

into light again embosoms and firmly establishes them in himself. For the demiurgus of the universe, though he is a divine intellect, yet he orderly arranges sensibles, and provides for subordinate natures. But the mighty Saturn is essentialized in separate intellections, and which transcend wholes. " For the fire which is beyond the first, says the Chaldean Oracle, does not incline its power downwards." But the demiurgus is suspended and proceeds from Saturn, being himself an intellect subsisting about an immaterial intellect, energizing about it as the intelligible, and producing that which is occult in it, into the apparent. For the maker of the world is an intellect of intellect. And it appears to me, that as Saturn is the summit of those Gods that are properly called intellectual, he is intellect, as with reference to the intelligible genus of Gods. For all the intellectual adhere to the intelligible genus of Gods, and are conjoined with them through intellections. " Ye who understand the supermundane paternal profundity," says the hymn to them. But Saturn is intelligible, with reference to all the intellectual Gods. *Purity*, therefore, indicates this impartible and imparticipable transcendency of Saturn. For the not coming into contact with matter, the impartible, and an exemption from habitude, are signified by purity. Such, indeed, is the transcendency of this God with respect to all coordination with things subordinate, and such his undefiled union with the intelligible, that he does not require a Curetic guard, like Rhea, Jupiter, and Proserpine. For all these, through their progressions into secondary natures, require the immutable defence of the Curetes. But Saturn being firmly established in himself, and hastily withdrawing himself from all subordinate natures, is established above the guardianship of the Curetes. He contains, however, the cause of these uniformly in himself. For this purity, and the undefiled which he possesses, give subsistence to all the progressions of the Curetes. Hence, in the Oracles, he is said to comprehend the first fountain of the Amilicti, and to ride on all the others. " The intellect of the father riding on attenuated rulers, they become refulgent with the furrows of inflexible and implacable fire."

Νους πατρος αραιοις εποχουμενος ιθυντηρσιν
Ακναμπτου αστραπτουσιν αμειλικτου πυρος ολκοις.

He is therefore *pure intellect*, as giving subsistence to the undefiled order, and as being the leader of the whole intellectual series.

Αυτου γαρ εκθρωσκουσιν αμειλικτοι τε κεραυνοι,
Και πρηστηροδοχοι κολποι παμφεγγεος αλκης·
Πατρογενους Εκατης, και υπεζωκος πυρος ανθος,
Ηδε κραταιον πνευμα πολων πυριων επεκεινα.

i. e. "From him leap forth the implacable thunders, and the prester-capacious bosoms of the all-splendid strength of the father-begotten Hecate, together with the environed flower of fire, and the strong spirit which is beyond the fiery poles."

For he convolves all the hebdomad of the fountains[16], and gives subsistence to it, from his unical and intelligible summit. For he is, as the Oracles say, αμισυλλευτος, uncut into fragments, uniform, and undistributed, and connectedly contains all the fountains, converting and uniting all of them to himself, and being separate from all things with immaculate purity. Hence he is κορονους, as an immaterial and pure intellect, and as establishing himself in the paternal silence. He is also celebrated as the father of fathers. Saturn, therefore, is a father, and intelligible, as with reference to the intellectual Gods.

Again, every intellect either abides, and is then intelligible, as being better than motion; or it is moved, and is then intellectual; or it is both, and is then intelligible, and at the same time intellectual. The first of these is Phanes;

---

[16] That is of the whole intellectual order, which consists of Saturn, Rhea, Jupiter, the three Curetes, and the separating monad Ocean.

the second, which is alone moved, is Saturn; and the third, which is both moved and permanent, is Heaven.

Saturn, from his impartible, unical, paternal, and beneficent subsistence in the intellectual orders, has been considered by some as the same with the one cause of all things. He is, however, only analogous to this cause, just as Orpheus calls the first cause *Time* (χρονος) nearly homonymously with Saturn (κρονος). But the Oracles of the Gods characterize this deity by the epithet of *the once* (τῳ απαξ); calling him *once beyond* (απαξ επικεινα). For *the once* is allied to *the one*.

Heaven, the father of Saturn, is an intellect understanding himself indeed, but united to the first intelligibles; in which he is also firmly established; and connectedly contains all the intellectual orders, by abiding in intelligible union. This God too is *connective*, just as Saturn is of a *separating* peculiarity; and on this account he is *father*. For connecting precede separating causes; and the intelligible and at the same time intellectual such as are intellectual only. Whence also *Heaven* being the *Synocheys* (συνοχευς) of wholes, according to one union gives subsistence to the Titannic series, and prior to this, to other orders of the Gods; some of which abide only in him, which he retains in himself; but others both abide and proceed, which he is said to have concealed after they were unfolded into light. And after all these, he gives subsistence to those divine orders which proceed into the universe, and are separated from their father. For he produces twofold monads, and triads, and hebdomads equal in number to the monads. These things, however, will be investigated more fully elsewhere. But this deity is denominated according to the similitude of the apparent Heaven. For each of them compresses and connects all the multitude which it contains, and causes the sympathy and connection of the whole world to be one. For connection is second to unifying power, and proceeds from it. In the Phædrus, therefore, Plato delivers to us the production of all secondary natures by Heaven, and shows us how this divinity leads upwards

ADDITIONAL NOTES. 179

and convolves all things to the intelligible. He likewise teaches us what its summit is, what the profundity of its whole order, and what the boundary of the whole of its progression. Here, therefore, investigating the truth of things from names, he declares its energy with respect to things more elevated and simple, and which are arranged nearer to *the one*. He also clearly appears here to consider the order of Heaven as intelligible and at the same time intellectual. For if it sees things on high, it energizes intellectually, and there is prior to it the intelligible genus of Gods, to which looking it is intellectual; just as it is intelligible to the natures which proceed from it. What then are the things on high which it beholds? Is it not evident that they are the supercelestial place, an essence without colour, without figure, and without the touch, and all the intelligible extent? An extent comprehending, as Plato would say, intelligible animals, the one cause of all eternal natures, and the occult principles of these; but, as the followers of Orpheus would say, bounded by æther upwards, and by Phanes downwards. For all between these two gives completion to the intelligible order. But Plato now calls this both singularly and plurally; since all things are there united, and at the same time each is separated peculiarly; and this according to the highest union and separation.

With respect to the term μετεωρολογοι, i. e. *those who discourse on sublime affairs*, we must now consider it in a manner adapted to those who choose an anagogic life, who live intellectually, and who do not gravitate to earth, but sublimely tend to a theoretic life. For that which is called Earth there maternally gives subsistence to such things as Heaven, which is coordinate to that Earth, produces paternally. And he who energizes there, may be properly called μετεωρολογος, or *one who discourses about things on high*. Heaven, therefore, being of a *connective* nature, is expanded above the Saturnian orders, and all the intellectual series; and produces from himself all the Titannic race; and prior to this, the perfective and defensive orders: and, in short, is the leader of every good to the intellectual Gods. Plato, therefore, having celebrated Saturn for his intelligence, which is without habitude to mundane natures; and for his life, which is converted to his own exalted place of survey, now celebrates Heaven for another more perfect energy. For to be conjoined to more elevated natures is a greater good than to be converted to oneself. Let no one however think, that on this account the abovementioned energies are distributed in the Gods; as, for instance, that there is providence alone in Jupiter, a conversion alone to himself in Saturn, and an elevation alone to the intelligible in Heaven. For Jupiter no otherwise provides for mundane natures than by looking to the intelligible; since, as Plato says in the Timæus, intellect understanding ideas in animal itself, thought it requisite that as many and such as it there perceived should be contained in the universe; but as Orpheus[17] says with a divinely inspired mouth, " Jupiter swallows his progenitor Phanes, embosoms all his powers, and becomes all things intellectually which Phanes is intelligibly." Saturn also imparts to Jupiter the principles of fabrication and of providential attention to sensibles, and understanding himself, he becomes united to first intelligibles, and is filled with the goods which are thence derived. Hence also the theologist (Orpheus) says " that he was nursed by Night[18]." If, therefore, the intelligible is nutriment, Saturn is replete not only with the intelligibles coordinated with him, but also with the highest and occult intellections. Heaven himself also fills all secondary natures with his proper goods, but guards all things by his own most vigorous powers; and the father supernally committed to him the connecting and guarding the causes of eternal animal. But he intellectually perceives himself, and is

---

[17] ως δ' Ορφευς ενθεω στοματι λεγει, και καταπινει τον προγονον αυτου τον φανητα, και συγκολπιζεται πασας αυτου τας δυναμεις ο ζευς, και γινεται παντα νοερως, οσαπερ ην εκεινος νοητως.

[18] διο και τρεφεσθαι φησιν αυτον ο θεολογος υπο της νυκτος. " εκ παντων δε κρονον νυξ ετρεφεν ηδ' απιταλλεν."

converted to the intelligibles which he contains; and this
his intelligence, Plato in the Phædrus calls *circulation*.
For as that which is moved in a circle is moved about its
own centre, so Heaven energizes about its own intelligible,
according to intellectual circulation. But all the Gods
subsisting in all, and each possessing all energies, one
transcends more in this, and another in a different energy,
and each is particularly characterized according to that in
which it transcends. Thus Jupiter is characterized by
providence, and hence his name is now thus analyzed;
but Saturn by a conversion to himself, whence also he is
inflected counsel, αγκυλομητις; and Heaven by habitude to
things more excellent; from which also he receives his
appellation. For his giving subsistence to a pure and the
Saturnian intellect represents his energy on the other part.
But as there are many powers in Heaven, such as the connective, guardian, and convertive, you will find that this
name is appropriately adapted to all these. For the connective is signified through bounding the intellectual Gods;
since the connective bounds the multitude which he contains. The power which guards wholes subsists through
the termination and security of an intellectual essence.
And the convertive power subsists through converting, seeing, and intellectually energizing natures, to things on high.
But all these are adapted to Heaven. For there is no fear
that the Gods will be dissipated, and that on this account
they require connective causes; or that they will sustain
mutation, and that on this account they stand in need of the
saving aid of guardian causes; but now Socrates at once
manifests all the powers of Heaven, through convertive
energy. For this is to behold things on high, to be converted to them, and through this to be connected and
defended. And it appears to me that Heaven possesses this
peculiarity according to analogy to the intelligible eternity
and the intelligible wholeness. For Timæus particularly
characterizes eternity by this, viz. by abiding in the one
prior to it, and by being established in the summit of intelligibles; and Socrates says that Heaven surveys things on

high, viz. the supercelestial place, and such things as are comprehended in the god-nourished silence of the fathers. (και οσα τη θεοθρεμμονι σιγη περιειληπται των πατερων). As, therefore, Parmenides signifies each of these orders through *wholeness*, the one through intelligible, and the other through intellectual wholeness; in like manner both Timæus and Socrates characterize them by a conversion to more excellent natures. But the conversion as well as the wholeness is different. For that of eternity is intelligible, on which account Timæus does not say that it looks to its intelligible, but only that it stably abides. But the conversion of Heaven is intellectual, and on this account Socrates says, that it sees things on high, and through this converts, guards, and connects all things posterior to itself. Whence also in the Phædrus, it is said by the circulation of itself, to lead all things to the supercelestial place, and the summit of the first intelligibles.

As there are three fathers and kings, of which Socrates here makes mention, Saturn alone appears to have received the government from his father, and to have transmitted it to Jupiter, by violence. Mythologists therefore celebrate the sections of Heaven and Saturn. But the cause of this is, that Heaven is of the connective, Saturn of the Titannic, and Jupiter of the demiurgic order. Again, the Titannic genus rejoices in separations and differences, progressions and multiplications of powers. Saturn, therefore, as a dividing God, separates his kingdom from that of Heaven; but as a pure intellect he is exempt from a fabricative energy proceeding into matter. Hence also the demiurgic genus is again separated from him. Section therefore is on both sides of him. For so far as he is a Titan, he is cut off from the connective causes, but so far as he does not give himself to material fabrication, he is cut off from the demiurgus Jupiter.

With respect, however, to the supercelestial place to which Heaven extends his intellectual life, some characterize it by ineffable symbols; but others, after giving it a name, celebrate it as unknown, neither being able to speak of its form or figure. And proceeding somewhat higher than this, they have been able to manifest the boundary [19] of the intelligible Gods by name alone. But the natures which are beyond this, they signify through analogy alone, these natures being ineffable and incomprehensible. Since that God who closes the paternal order is said by the wise to be the only deity among the intelligible Gods, that is denominated: and theurgy ascends as far as to this order. Since, therefore, the natures prior to Heaven are allotted such a transcendency of uniform subsistence that some of them are said to be effable, and at the same time ineffable, known, and at the same time unknown, through their alliance to *the one*, Socrates very properly restrains the discourse about them, in consequence of names not being able to represent their hyparxis; and, in short, because it requires a certain wonderful employment to separate the effable and ineffable, of their hyparxis or power. He accuses, therefore, his memory, not as disbelieving in the fables, which assert that there are certain more ancient causes beyond Heaven, nor as not thinking it worth while to mention them. For in the Phædrus he himself celebrates the supercelestial place. But he says this, because the first of beings cannot become known by the exercise of memory and through phantasy, or opinion, or the dianoetic part. For we are alone naturally adapted to be be conjoined to them, with the flower of intellect and the hyparxis of our essence; and through these we receive the sensation of their unknown nature. Socrates therefore says, that what in them is exempt, both from our gnostic and recollective life, is the cause of our inability to give them a name; for they are not naturally adapted to be known through names. Theologists, likewise, would not remotely signify them, and through the analogy of things apparent to them, if they could be named, and apprehended by knowledge.

[19] That is Phanes, intelligible intellect, or in the language of Plato αυτοζωον, *animal* itself.

Homer[20] does not ascend beyond the Saturnian order, but evincing that Saturn is the proximate cause of the demiurgus, he calls Jupiter, who is the demiurgus, the son of Saturn. He also calls the divinities coordinate with him Juno, Neptune, and Mars; and he denominates Jupiter the father of men and Gods. But he does not introduce Saturn as either energizing or saying any thing but as truly αγκυλομητις, in consequence of being converted to himself.

Orpheus greatly availed himself of the license of fables, and manifests every thing prior to Heaven by names, as far as to the first cause. He also denominates the ineffable who transcends the intelligible unities, *Time;* whether because *Time* presubsists as the cause of all generation, or because, as delivering the generation of true beings, he thus denominates the ineffable, that he may indicate the order of true beings, and the transcendency of the more total to the more partial; that a subsistence according to Time may be the same with a subsistence according to cause; in the same manner as generation with an arranged progression. But Hesiod venerates many of the divine natures in silence, and does not in short name the first. For that what is posterior to the first proceeds from something else, is evident from the verse,

" Chaos of all things was the first produced."

For it is perfectly impossible that it could be produced without a cause; but he does not say what that is which gave subsistence to Chaos. He is silent indeed with respect to both the fathers[21] of intelligibles, the exempt, and the coordinate; for they are perfectly ineffable. And with

[20] Homer, however, appears to have ascended as far as to the Goddess Night, or the summit of the intelligible and at the same time intellectual order.

[21] That is to say, *the first cause, and bound* which is called by Orpheus *æther.*

respect to the two coordinations, the natures which are coordinate with the one, he passes by in silence, but those alone which are coordinate with the indefinite duad, he unfolds through genealogy. And on this account Plato now thinks Hesiod deserves to be mentioned, for passing by the natures prior to Heaven, as being ineffable. For this also is indicated concerning them by the Oracles, which likewise add, " they possess mystic silence." And Socrates himself, in the Phædrus, calls the intellectual perception of them μυησις and εποπτεια, *in which nearly the whole business is ineffable and unknown.*

The theology of Hesiod from the monad Rhea produces, according to things which are more excellent in the coordination, Vesta; but according to those which are subordinate, Juno; and according to those which subsist between, Ceres. But according to Orpheus, Ceres is in a certain respect the same with the whole of vivification, and in a certain respect is not the same. For on high she is Rhea, but below, in conjunction with Jupiter, she is Ceres: for here the things begotten are similar to the begetters, and are nearly the same.

Again, we ought to receive with caution what is now said concerning effluxions and motions. For Socrates does not descend to the material flowing of Heraclitus; for this is false[22], and unworthy the dianoetic conceptions of Plato. But since it is lawful to interpret things divine analogously, through appropriate images, Socrates very properly assimilates fontal and Saturnian deities to streams; in so doing jesting and at the same time acting seriously, because good is always derived as it were in streams from on high, to things below. Hence, according to the image of rivers, after the fontal deities, who eternally devolve streams of good, the deities who subsist as principles are

---

[22] That is to say, it is false to assert of intellectual and divine natures, that they are in a perpetual flux; for they are eternally stable themselves, and are the sources of stability to other things.

celebrated. For after the *fountain* of a river the place where it *begins* to flow is surveyed.

But those divinities who are peculiarly denominated total intellectual Gods, of whom the great Saturn is the father, are properly called fontal. For "from him leap forth the implacable thunders," says the Oracle concerning Saturn. But concerning the vivific fountain Rhea, from which all life, divine, intellectual, psychical, and mundane is generated, the Chaldean Oracles thus speak,

Ρειη τοι νοερων μακαρων πηγη τε ροη τε.
Παντων γαρ πρωτη δυναμεις κολποισιν αφραστοις
Δεξαμενη, γενεην επι παν προχεει τροχαουσαν.

i. e. "Rhea [23] is the fountain and river of the blessed intellectual Gods. For first receiving the powers of all things in her ineffable bosoms, she pours running generation into every thing."

For this divinity gives subsistence to the infinite diffusion of all life, and to all never failing powers. She likewise moves all things according to the measures of divine motions, and converts them to herself; establishing all things in herself, as being coordinate to Saturn. Rhea, therefore, is so called from causing a perpetual influx of good, and through being the cause of divine *facility*, since the life of the gods is attended with *ease* (θεοι ρεια ζωντες).

Ocean is the cause to all the Gods of acute and vigorous energy, and bounds the separations of the first, middle, and last orders; converting himself to himself, and to his proper principles, through swiftness of intellect, but moving all things from himself, to energies accommodated to their natures; perfecting their powers, and causing them to have a never failing subsistence. But Tethys imparts permanency to the natures which are moved by Ocean, and

---

[23] Gesner, misled by Patricius, has inserted these lines among the Orphic fragments, in his edition of the works of Orpheus.

stability to the beings which are excited by him to the generation of secondary natures. She is also the source of purity of essence to those beings who perpetually desire to produce all things; as sustaining every thing in the divine essences which, as it were, *leaps forth and percolates.* For each of first causes, though it imparts to secondary natures a participation of good, yet at the same time retains with itself that which is undefiled, unmingled, and pure from participation. Thus, for instance, intellect is filled with life, being, and intelligence, with which also it fills soul; but establishing in itself that which in each of these is genuine and exempt, it also illuminates from itself to beings of a subordinate rank, inferior measures of these goods. And vigour of energy, indeed, is present with more ancient natures, through Ocean; but the leaping forth and percolating through Tethys. For every thing which is imparted from superior to subordinate natures, whether it be essence, life, or intelligence, is *percolated*. And such of these as are primary are established in themselves; but such as are more imperfect are transferred to things of a subject order. Just as with respect to streams of water, such of them as are nearer their source are purer, but the more remote are more turbid. Both Ocean and Tethys, therefore, are fontal Gods, according to their first subsistence. Hence Socrates now calls them the fathers of streams. But they also proceed into other orders of Gods, exhibiting the same powers among the Gods who rank as principles or rulers, among those of a liberated, and those of a celestial characteristic; and appropriately in each of these. Timæus, however, celebrates their sublunary orders, calling them fathers of Saturn and Rhea, but the progeny of Heaven and Earth. But their last processions are their divisible allotments about the earth; both those which are apparent on its surface, and those which under the earth separate the kingdom of Hades from the dominion of Neptune.

Saturn is conjoined both to Rhea and Jupiter, but to the

former as father to prolific power, but to the latter as father to intelligible [24] intellect.

Ocean is said to have married Tethys, and Jupiter Juno, and the like, as establishing a communion with her, conformably to the generation of subordinate natures. For an according coarrangement of the Gods, and a connascent cooperation in their productions, is called by theologists *marriage*.

Tethys is denominated from leaping forth and *straining or cleansing*, being as it were *Diatethys*, and by taking away the first two syllables *Tethys* [25].

Saturn is the monad of the Titannic order of the Gods, but Jupiter of the demiurgic. This last divinity, however, is twofold, the one exempt and coordinated with Saturn, being a fontal God, and, in short, ranking with the intellectual fathers, and convolving the extremity of them; but the other being connumerated with the sons of Saturn, and allotted a Saturnian summit and dominion in this triad; concerning which also the Homeric Neptune says,

τρεις γαρ τ' εκ Κρονου ειμεν αδελφεοι, ους τεκε Ρειη [26].

As brother Gods we three from Saturn came,
And Rhea bore us.

And the first Jupiter indeed, as being the demiurgus of wholes, is the king of things first, middle, and last, concerning whom Socrates also had just said, that he is the ruler and king of all things; and life and salvation are imparted to all things through him.

---

[24] Proclus here means that there is the same analogy between Saturn, Rhea, and Jupiter, as in the intelligible triad, between father, power, and intellect.

[25] Οτι ωνομασται η Τηθυς παρα το διαττομενον και ηθουμενον, οιον Διατηθυς, και αφαιρετει των πρωτων δισυλλαβων Τηθυς.

[26] Iliad, xiv. 187.

But the ruling Jupiter, who ranks as a principle, and who is coordinate with the three sons of Saturn, governs the third part of the whole of things, according to that of Homer,

τριχθα δε παντα δεδασται——[27].

A triple distribution all things own.

He is also the summit of the three, has the same name with the fontal Jupiter, is united to him, and is monadically called Jupiter. But the second is called dyadically, marine Jupiter, and Neptune. And the third is triadically denominated terrestrial Jupiter, Pluto, and Hades. The first of these also preserves, fabricates, and vivifies summits, but the second, things of a second rank, and the third those of a third order. Hence this last is said to have ravished Proserpine, that together with her he might animate the extremities of the universe.

The Titannic order dividing itself from the connecting order of Heaven, but having also something in itself abiding, and connascent with that order, Saturn is the leader of the separation, and on this account he both arms others against his father, and receives the scythe [28] from his mother, through which he divides his own kingdom from that of Heaven. But Ocean is coordinated with those that abide in the manners of the father, and guards the middle of the two orders; so far as a Titan being connumerated with the Gods that subsist with Saturn; but so far as rejoicing in a coordination with Heaven, conjoining himself with the Synoches. For it is fit that he who bounds the first and second orders should be arranged in the middle of the natures that are bounded. But every where this God is allotted a power of this kind, and separates the genera of the Gods, the Titannic from the connecting (των συνοχικων), and the vivific from the demiurgic. Whence also ancient rumour calls Ocean the God who separates the apparent

---

[27] Iliad xv. 189.   [28] See the Theogony of Hesiod, v. 176, &c.

part of Heaven from the unapparent; and on this account poets say, that the sun and the other stars rise from the ocean. What is now said therefore by Plato, comprehends all the Titannic order through these two conjunctions; this order abiding, and at the same time proceeding. And through the Saturnian order, indeed, it comprehends every thing separated from the fathers; but through that of Ocean, every thing conjoined with the connecting Gods. Or if you had rather so speak, through the Saturnian order, he comprehends every maternal cause, but through the other, every thing subservient to the paternal cause. For the female is the cause of progression and separation, but the male of union and stable permanency.

Of the demiurgic triad [29] which divides the whole world, and distributes the indivisible, one, and whole fabrication of the first Jupiter, the summit, and which has the relation of father, is Jupiter, who, through union with the whole demiurgic intellect having the same appellation with it, is for this reason not mentioned here by Plato. But Neptune is allotted the middle, and that which binds together both the extremes; being filled indeed from the essence of Jupiter, but filling Pluto. For of the whole of this triad, Jupiter indeed is the father, but Neptune the power, and Pluto the intellect. And all, indeed, are in all; but each receives a different character of subsistence. Thus Jupiter subsists according to *being;* but Neptune according to *power,* and Pluto according to *intellect.* And though all these divinities are the causes of the life of all things, yet one is so *essentially,* another *vitally,* and another *intellectually.* Whence also the theologist Orpheus says, that the extremes fabricate in conjunction with Proserpine things first and last; the middle being coarranged with generative cause from his own allotment, without Proserpine. Hence *violence* is said to have been offered to Proserpine by Jupiter; but she is said to have been *ravished* by Pluto (διο και

---

[29] That is, of the first triad of the supermundane, which subsists immediately after the intellectual order.

φασι την κορην υπο μεν του διος βιαζεσθαι, υπο δε του πλουτωνος αρπαζεσθαι). But the middle is said to be the cause of motion to all things. Hence, also, he is called *earth-shaker*, as being the origin of motion. And among those who are allotted the kingdom of Saturn, the middle allotment, and the agile sea (η ευκινητος θαλασσα) are assigned to him. According to every division, therefore, the summits are Jovian, the middles belong to Neptune, and the extremes to Pluto. And if you look to the centres, such as the east, that of mid-heaven, and the west; if also you divide the whole world, as for instance into the inerratic, planetary, and sublunary spheres;—or again, if you divide that which is generated into the fiery, terrestrial, and that which subsists between; or the earth into its summits, middle, and hollow, and subterranean parts, this triad every where distributes the first, middle, and last differences of things fabricated in demiurgic boundaries.

The name Neptune is now triply analyzed. For Neptune is the trident-bearer; and the Tritons and Amphitrite are the familiars of this God. And the first analyzation of his name is from the allotment over which he presides, and from souls coming into generation, in whom the circle of sameness is fettered; since the sea is analogous to generation. But the second is from communion with the first.

αλλα ζευς προτερος γεγονει, και πλειονα ηδει [30].

But Jove was born the first, and more he knows.

For a Jupiter of this kind is the proximate intelligible of Neptune. But the third analysis of his name is from his energy in externals. For he is motive of nature, and vivific of things last. He is also the guardian of the earth, and excites it to generations.

Neptune is an intellectual demiurgic God, who receives souls descending into generation; but Hades is an intellectual demiurgic God, who frees souls from generation. For

[30] Hom. Iliad.

as our whole period receives a triple division, into a life prior to generation, which is Jovian, into a life in generation, which is Neptunian, and into a life posterior to generation, which is Plutonian; Pluto, who is characterized by intellect, very properly converts ends to beginnings, effecting a circle without a beginning and without an end, not only in souls, but also in every fabrication of bodies, and in short, of all periods;—which circle also he perpetually convolves. Thus for instance, he converts the ends to the beginnings of the souls of the stars, and the convolutions of souls about generation, and the like. And hence Jupiter is the guardian of the life of souls prior to generation.

Some, however, badly analyze the name of Pluto into wealth from the earth, through fruits and metals; but Hades into the invisible, dark, and dreadful. These Socrates now reprobates, bringing the two names to the same signification; referring the name of Pluto, as intellect, to the wealth of prudence, but that of Hades to an intellect knowing all things. For this God is a sophist, who, purifying souls after death, frees them from generation. For Hades is not, as some improperly explain it, evil: for neither is death evil; though Hades to some appears to be attended with perturbations ($\epsilon\mu\pi a\theta\omega\varsigma$); but it is invisible, and better than the apparent; such as is every thing intelligible. Intellect, therefore, in every triad of beings, convolves itself to being, and the paternal cause, imitating in its energy the circle.

Men who are lovers of body badly refer to themselves the passions of the animated nature, and on this account consider death to be dreadful, as being the cause of corruption. The truth, however, is, that it is much better for man to die, and live in Hades a life according to nature, since a life in conjunction with body is contrary to nature, and is an impediment to intellectual energy. Hence it is necessary to divest ourselves of the fleshly garments with which we are clothed, as Ulysses did of his ragged vestments, and no longer like a wretched mendicant, together with the indigence of body, put on our rags. For, as the Chaldean Oracle says, " Things divine cannot be obtained by those whose intellectual eye is directed to body; but those only can arrive at the possession of them who stript of their garments hasten to the summit."

Neptune, when compared with Jupiter, is said to know *many* things; but Hades, compared with souls to whom he imparts knowledge, is said to know *all* things; though Neptune is more total than Hades.

As it is necessary to analyze Pluto, not only into the obvious wealth from the earth, but also into the wealth of wisdom, so likewise Ceres must be analyzed not only into corporeal nutriment; but beginning from the Gods themselves it is requisite to conceive her to be the supplier of aliment, first to the Gods themselves, afterwards to the natures posterior to the Gods; and in the last place, that the series of this beneficent energy extends as far as to corporeal nutriment. For the characteristic of love shines forth first of all in the Gods; and this is the case with the medicinal and prophetic powers of Apollo, and with those of every other divinity. But nutriment, when considered with reference to the Gods, is the communication of intellectual plenitude from more exalted natures to those of an inferior rank. Gods, therefore, are nourished, when they view with the eye of intellect Gods prior to themselves; and when they are perfected and view intelligible beauties, such as justice itself, temperance itself, and the like, as it is said in the Phædrus.

From sportive conceptions about the Gods, it is possible for those to energize entheastically, or according to a divinely inspired energy, who apply themselves to things in a more intellectual manner. Thus, for instance, according to the material conceptions of the multitude, Venus derives her origin from foam; and foam corresponds to seed. Hence, according to them, the pleasure arising from this in coition is Venus. Who, however, is so stupid as not to survey primary and eternal natures, prior to such as are last and corruptible? I will therefore unfold the divine conception respecting Venus.

They say then that the first Venus was produced from twofold causes, the one as that *through which*[31], cooperating with her progression, as calling forth the prolific power of the father, and imparting it to the intellectual orders; but Heaven as the maker and cause unfolding the goddess into light, from his own generative abundance. For whence could that which congregates different genera, according to one desire of beauty, receive its subsistence except from the *synochical* power of Heaven? From the foam, therefore, of his own prolific parts thrown into the sea, Heaven produced this Goddess, as Orpheus says. But the second Venus Jupiter produces from his own generative powers, in conjunction with Dione; and this goddess likewise proceeds from foam, after the same manner with the more ancient Venus, as Orpheus evinces. These goddesses therefore differ from each other, according to the causes of their production, their orders and their powers. For she that proceeds from the genitals of Heaven is supermundane, leads upwards to intelligible beauty, is the supplier of an unpolluted life, and separates from generation. But the Venus that proceeds from Dione governs all the coordinations in the celestial world and the earth, binds them to each other, and perfects their generative progressions, through a kindred conjunction. These divinities too are united with each other through a similitude of subsistence: for they both proceed from generative powers; one from that of the connectedly containing power of Heaven, and the other from Jupiter the demiurgus. But the sea signifies an expanded and circumscribed life; its profundity, the universally extended progression of such a life; and its foam, the greatest purity of nature, that which is full of prolific light and power, and that which swims upon all life, and is as it were its highest flower.

According to Orpheus, Ceres is the same with Rhea. For he says, that subsisting on high in unproceeding union

---

[31] This cause is Saturn, who according to the fable cut off the genital parts of Heaven. See the Theogony of Hesiod.

with Saturn, she is *Rhea*, but that by emitting and generating Jupiter, she is *Ceres*. For thus he speaks,

Ρειην το πριν εουσαν, επει διος επλετο μητηρ
Γεγονε δημητηρ [32].

i. e. The goddess who was *Rhea*, when she bore Jove became Ceres.

But Hesiod says that Ceres is the daughter of Rhea. It is however evident that these theologists harmonize: for whether this goddess proceeds from union with Saturn to a secondary order, or whether she is the first progeny of Rhea, she is still the same. Ceres, therefore, thus subsisting, and receiving the most ancient and ruling order from the whole vivific Rhea (της ολης ζωογονον ρεας), and comprehending the middle centres of whole vivification (της ολης ζωογονιας), she fills all supermundane natures with the rivers of all-perfect life, pouring upon all things vitally, indivisibly, and uniformly.

Prior however to all this, she unfolds to us the demiurgic intellect (Jupiter), and imparts to him the power of vivifying wholes. For as Saturn supplies her from on high with the cause of being; so Ceres from on high, and from her own prolific bosoms, pours forth vivification to the demiurgus. But possessing herself the middle of all vivific deity, she governs the whole fountains which she contains, and comprehends the one bond of the first and last powers of life. She stably convolves too, and contains all secondary fountains. But she leads forth the uniform causes of prior natures to the generation of others. This goddess too comprehends *Vesta* and *Juno:* in her right hand parts Juno, who pours forth the whole order of souls; but in her left hand parts Vesta, who leads forth all the light of virtue. Hence Ceres is with great propriety called by

---

[32] This Orphic fragment is not to be found in Gesner's or Hermann's collection of the Orphic remains.

Plato[23] *mother*, and at the same time the *supplier of aliment*. For, so far as she comprehends in herself the cause of Juno, she is a mother; but as containing Vesta in her essence, she is the supplier of aliment. But the paradigm of this goddess is *Night: for immortal Night is called the nurse of the Gods.* Night however is the cause of aliment intelligibly[24]: for that which is intelligible is, according to the oracle[25], the aliment of the intellectual orders of Gods. But Ceres first of all separates the two kinds of aliment in the Gods, as Orpheus says:

Μησατο γαρ προπολους, και αμφιπολους, και οπαδους·
Μησατο δ' αμβροσιην, και ερυθρον νεκταρος αρθρον
Μησατο δ' αγλαα εργα μελισσαων εριβομβων[26].

i. e. She cares for pow'rs ministrant, whether they
Or Gods *precede*, or *follow*, or *surround:*
Ambrosia, and *tenacious nectar red*
Are too the objects of her bounteous care.
Last to the bee her providence extends,
Who gathers honey with resounding hum.

Ceres, therefore, our sovereign mistress (δεσποινα) not only generates life, but that which gives perfection to life; and this from supernal natures to such as are last: *for virtue is the perfection of souls.* Hence mothers who are connected with the circulations of time, bring forth their offspring in imitation of this twofold and eternal generation of Ceres. For, at the same time that they send forth their young into the light, they extend to them milk naturally produced as their food.

Again, the conjunction of the demiurgic intellect with

[23] See p. 521, vol. v. of my Translation of Plato.

[24] Because Night subsists at the summit of *the intelligible and at the same time intellectual* order, and is wholly absorbed in the intelligible.

[25] That is, according to one of the Chaldean Oracles.

[26] These verses likewise are not in Gesner's and Hermann's collection.

ADDITIONAL NOTES. 197

the vivific causes is triple: for it is conjoined with the fountains prior to itself: is present with its kindred coordinate natures; and coenergizes with the orders posterior to itself. For it is present with the mother prior to itself, *convertively* (ἐπιστρεπτικως); with Proserpine posterior to itself, *providentially* (προνοητικως); and with Juno coordinate to itself with an *amatory energy* (ερασμιως). Hence Jupiter is said to be enamoured of Juno,

ως σεο νυν εραμαι[27].

As now I love thee,——

And this love indeed is legal, but the other two appear to be illegal. This Goddess therefore produces from herself, in conjunction with the demiurgus and father, all the genera of souls, the supermundane and mundane, the celestial and sublunary, the divine, angelic, dæmoniacal, and partial. After a certain manner too, she is divided from the demiurgus, but in a certain respect she is united to him: for Jupiter is said, in the Philebus, to contain a royal intellect and a royal soul. For he contains uniformly the paternal and maternal cause of the world; and the fountain of souls is said to be in Jupiter; just as again the intelligence of Jupiter is said to be first participated by Juno. For no other divinity, says Jupiter in Homer, knows my mind prior to Juno. Through this ineffable union therefore of these divinities, the world participates of intellectual souls. They also give subsistence to intellects who are carried in souls, and who together with them give completion to the whole fabrication of things.

The series of our sovereign mistress Juno, beginning from on high, pervades to the last of things; and her allotment in the sublunary region is the air. For *air* is a symbol of *soul,* according to which also soul is called a *spirit* (πνευμα); just as *fire* is an image of *intellect,* but *water* of *nature,* by which the world is nourished (της κοσ-

---

[27] Iliad, xiv. 328.

μοτροφου φυσεως), through which all nutriment and increase are produced. But *earth* is the image of *body*, through its gross and material nature. Hence Homer, obscurely signifying this, represents Juno suspended with two anvils under her feet: for the air is allotted two heavy elements beneath itself.

For

ηλιον δ' ακαμαντα βοωπις ποτνια ηρη
πεμψεν επ' ωκεανοιο ροας.

i. e. "Fair-eyed venerable Juno sent the sun to the streams of the ocean,"—is from the same conception.

For he calls the thick cloud produced by Juno the setting of the sun. The assertion likewise that the end of this name will be conjoined with the beginning, if any one frequently repeats the name of the Goddess, evinces the conversion of rational souls to her which proceed from her; and that voice is air that is struck. On this account also the voice of rational animals is especially dedicated to this Goddess, who made the horse of Achilles to become vocal. But Socrates now delivers these three vivific monads in a consequent order, viz. Ceres, Juno, Proserpine; calling the first the mother, the second the sister, and the third the daughter of the demiurgus. All of them however are partakers of the whole of fabrication; the first in an exempt manner and intellectually, the second in a fontal manner, and at the same time in a way adapted to a principle (αρχικως), and the third in a manner adapted to a principle and leader (αρχικως και ηγεμονικως).

Of these Goddesses the last possesses triple powers, and impartibly and uniformly comprehends three monads of Gods. But she is called Core (κορη) through the purity of her essence, and her undefiled transcendency in her generations. She also possesses a first, middle, and last empire. And according to her summit, indeed, she is called Diana by Orpheus; but according to her middle Proserpine; and according to the extremity of the order Minerva. Likewise, according to an hyparxis transcending the other

ADDITIONAL NOTES. 199

powers of this triple vivific order, the dominion of Hecate is established; but according to a middle power, and which is generative of wholes, that of Soul; and according to intellectual conversion that of Virtue [38]. Core therefore, subsisting on high, and among the supermundane Gods, uniformly extends this triple order of divinities; and together with Jupiter generates Bacchus, who impartibly presides over partible fabrication. But beneath, in conjunction with Pluto, she is particularly beheld according to the middle peculiarity; for it is this which proceeding every where imparts vivification to the last of things. Hence she is called Proserpine, because she especially associates with Pluto, and together with him orderly distributes the extremities of the universe. And according to her extremities indeed, she is said to be a virgin, and to remain undefiled: but according to her middle, to be conjoined with Hades, and to beget the Furies in the subterranean regions. She therefore is also called Core, but after another manner than the supermundane and ruling Core. For the one is the connective unity of the three vivific principles; but the other is the middle of them, in herself possessing the peculiarities of the extremes. Hence in the Proserpine conjoined with Pluto, you will find the peculiarities of Hecate and Minerva; but these extremes subsist in her occultly, while the peculiarity of the middle shines forth, and that which is characteristic of ruling soul, which in the supermundane Core was of a *ruling* [39] nature, but here subsists according to a mundane peculiarity.

Proserpine is denominated, either through judging of forms and separating them from each other, thus obscurely signifying the ablation of slaughter (δια το κρινειν τα ειδη και χωριζειν. αλληλων, ως του φονου την αναιρεσιν αινιττομε-

---

[38] Proclus says this conformably to the theology of the Chaldeans. For according to that theology, the first monad of the vivific triad is *Hecate*, the second *Soul*, and the third *Virtue*.

[39] That is, of a supermundane nature: for the *ruling* are the *supermundane* Gods.

νον), or through separating souls perfectly from bodies, through a conversion to things on high, which is the most fortunate slaughter and death, to such as are worthy of it (η δια το χωριζειν τας ψυχας τελεως εκ των σωματων δια της προς τα ανω επιστροφης, οπερ εστιν ευτυχεστατος φονος και θανατος τοις αξιουμενοις τουτου). But the name φερεφαττα, *Pherephatta*, according to a contract with generation, is adapted to Proserpine; but according to wisdom and counsel to Minerva. At the same time, however, all the appellations by which she is distinguished are adapted to the perfection of soul. On this account also she is called Proserpine, and not by the names of the extremes; since that which was ravished by Pluto is the middle; the extremes at the same time being firmly established in themselves, according to which Core is said to remain a virgin.

With respect to our sovereign mistress Diana, Plato delivers three peculiarities of her, the undefiled, the mundane, and the anagogic. And through the first of these indeed, the goddess is said to be a lover of virginity; but through the second, according to which she is perfective of works (τελεσιουργος) she is said to be the inspective guardian of virtue; and through the third she is said to hate the impulses arising from generation. Of these three, likewise, the first is especially adapted to the progression of the goddess, according to which she is allotted an hyparxis in the vivific triad of the supermundane Gods; whether we call this deity Hecatic, as Theurgists say, or Diana with Orpheus. For there being established, she is filled with undefiled powers from the Gods called *Amilicti*[40]. But she looks to the fountain of virtue, and embraces its virginity. For the virginity which is there does not proceed forth, as the Oracle says, but abiding gives subsistence to Diana, and to supermundane virtue, and is exempt from all communion, conjunction, and progression, according to generation. Hence Core also, according to the

[40] That is, the Corybantes.

Diana and Minerva which she contains, is said to remain a virgin; but according to the prolific power of Proserpine, she is said to proceed forth, and to be conjoined with the third demiurgus, and to bring forth, as Orpheus says, "nine azure-eyed, flower-producing daughters;"

εννεα θυγατερας γλαυκωπιδας ανθεσιουργους·

since the Diana and the Minerva which she contains preserve their virginity always the same. For the former of these is characterized according to her stability, but the latter according to her convertive energy. But that which is generative is allotted in her a middle order. They say too, that she aspires after virginity, since the form of her is comprehended in the vivific fountain, and she understands fontal virtue, gives subsistence to supermundane and anagogic virtue, and despises all material sexual connexion, though she inspects the fruits arising from it.

She appears also to be averse to the generations and progressions of things, but to introduce perfections to them. And she gives perfection indeed to souls through a life according to virtue; but to mortal animals she imparts a restitution to form. But that there is a great union between Diana, the mundane Hecate, and Core, is evident to those that are in the least degree conversant with the writings of Orpheus; from which it appears that Latona is comprehended in Ceres, and together with Jupiter gives subsistence to Core, and the mundane Hecate. To which we may also add, that Orpheus [41] calls Diana Hecate. So that it is nothing wonderful, if we should elsewhere call the Diana contained in Core Hecate.

The wise man venerates the last and mundane progressions of the Gods, though, as Plato says, they are sports through these Gods [i. e. Venus and Bacchus] being lovers of sport. For as he says of the terminations of the other Gods, that they are terrible, and that they avenge and

---

[41] Η δ' αρα εκαστη παιδος μελη ανδα λυπουσα
Λητους ευπλοκαμοιο κορη προτεθησατ' ολυμπον.

punish, and thus give perfection to souls; as for instance, that Justice follows Jupiter, the avenger of the divine law, and that this divinity is benevolent to those whose manners are orderly, and who live according to intellect; but that she is baneful to those who mingle their life with insolence and ignorance, until she has entirely subverted them, their houses, and cities;—in like manner, he venerates the terminations of Bacchus and Venus, which produce γλνευ-θυμια, *sweetness of sensation;* every where purifying our conceptions concerning the Gods, and preparing us to understand that all things look to the best end, whatever it may be. For because the terminations of these divinities strengthen the infirmity of the mortal nature, and recall corporeal molestation, on this account the Gods, the causes of these things, are φιλοπαιγμονες, *lovers of sport.* Hence of statues, they make some of them laughing and dancing, and exhibiting relaxation, but others austere, astonishing and terrible to the view, analagously to the mundane allotments of the Gods.

That theologists frequently call Bacchus *wine,* from the last of his gifts, as for instance Orpheus,

οινου παντα μελη κοσμω λαβε, και μοι ενεικε.

i. e. " Take all the members of wine (that are distributed) in the world and bring them to me."

But if the God is thus denominated, certainly his first and middle energies will be thus called, as well as his last; so that Socrates now looking to this, calls the God διδοινυσος, beginning from wine, which, as we have said, manifests all the powers of the God. Thus also in the Phædrus, Socrates calls love in common *great,* both that which is divine and that which is a lover of body. By this epithet *wine,* therefore, we must understand that the peculiarity of a partial intellect is in common presented to our view. For the word οιουν, *such as,* is nothing else than intellectual form separated from a total intellect, and in consequence of this becoming participated, *particular* and *alone.*

For an all-perfect intellect is all things, and energizes according to all things with invariable sameness; but a partial and participated intellect is indeed all things, but this according to one form, such as a solar, lunar, or mercurial form. This therefore, the peculiarity of which is to be separated from the rest, wine indicates, signifying an intellect *such as* and *particular* (σημαινων τον οιον και τινα νουν). Since therefore every partial fabrication is suspended from the Dionysiacal monad, which distributes participated mundane intellects from total intellect [or the intellect which ranks as a whole], many souls from one soul, and all sensible forms from their proper totalities; on this account theologists call both this God and all his fabrications *wine*. For all these are the progeny of intellect; and some things participate of the partial distribution of intellect in a more distant, but others in a nearer degree. *Wine* therefore energizes in things analogously to its subsistence in them; in body, indeed, after the manner of an image, according to a false opinion and imagination; but in intellectual natures according to an intellectual energy and fabrication; since in the laceration of Bacchus by the Titans, the heart of the God [i. e. the indivisible essence of intellect] is said to have alone remained undistributed.

Again, theologists especially celebrate two powers of our sovereign mistress Minerva, the *defensive* and the *perfective;* the former preserving the order of wholes undefiled, and unvanquished by matter, and the latter filling all things with intellectual light, and converting them to their cause. And on this account, Plato also in the Timæus, analogously celebrates Minerva as *philopolemic* and *philosophic*. But three orders of this Goddess are delivered by theologists; the one fontal and intellectual, according to which she establishes herself in her father Jupiter, and subsists in unproceeding union with him; but the second ranks among the supermundane Gods, according to which she is present with Core, and bounds and converts all the progression of that Goddess to herself. And the third is *liberated*, according to which she perfects and guards the whole world, and circularly invests it with her powers, as with a veil; binding together all the mundane summits, and giving subsistence to all the allotments in the heavens, and to those which proceed into the sublunary region. Now therefore Socrates celebrates her *guardian* power, through the name of *Pallas;* but her *perfective* power through that of *Minerva.* She is the cause therefore of orderly and measured motion, which she first imparts to the Curetic order, and afterwards to the other Gods. For Minerva, according to this power, is the leader of the Curetes, as Orpheus says, whence also, as well as those divinities she is adorned with empyrean arms, through which she represses all disorder, preserves the demiurgic series immovable, and unfolds dancing through rythmical motion. She also guards reason as it proceeds from intellect; through this power vanquishing matter. For the visible region, says Timæus, is mingled from intellect and necessity, the latter being obedient to the former, and all material causes being in subjection to the will of the father. It is this Goddess therefore who arranges necessity under the productions of intellect, raises the universe to the participation of Jupiter, excites and establishes it in the port of its father, and eternally guards and defends it. Hence, if the universe is said to be indissoluble, it is this goddess who supplies its permanency; and if it moves in measured motion, through the whole of time, according to one reason and order, she is the source of this supply. She watchfully surveys therefore all the fabrication of her father, and connects and converts it to him; and vanquishes all material indefiniteness. Hence she is called *Victory* and *Health;* the former because she causes intellect to rule over necessity, and form over matter; and the latter, because she preserves the world[42] perpetually whole, perfect, exempt

---

[42] In the very learned Professor Boissonade's edition of this work, for τον κοσμον in this place, there is nothing more than το κον; and my manuscript has very erroneously το κακον. But the true reading is undoubtedly τον κοσμον. For Proclus, in what he here says, alludes to the following

ADDITIONAL NOTES. 205

from age, and free from disease. It is the property therefore of this Goddess to elevate and distribute, and through an intellectual dance as it were, to connect, establish, and defend inferior natures in such as are more divine [43].

words of Plato in the Timæus, δια δε την αιτιαν και τον λογισμον τονδε, εν ολον εξ απαντων τελεον και αγηρων και ανοσον αυτον [i. e. τον κοσμον] ετεχνατο. In all the editions of Plato's works, however, there is a very erroneous omission in this passage. For from the text of Proclus, and also from what Plato previously says, instead of εν ολον εξ απαντων, it is necessary to read εν ολον εξ ολων απαντων. And then the passage will be in English, "Through this cause, and from this reasoning process he [i. e. the Demiurgus] fashioned the world one perfect whole, consisting of all wholes, exempt from age and free from disease."

[43] The whole of this sentence is in my manuscript as follows: Οικειον ουν της θεου ταυτης και το αναγειν και μεριζειν, και δια της νοερας Χορειας συναπτειν τοις θειοτεροις, και ενδρυειν και φρουρειν εν αυτοις. But after the word μεριζειν, it is necessary either to add or conceive to be implied τα εαυτης. The last word, αυτοις, is wanting in the Professor's edition.

THE END.

C. Whittingham, College House, Chiswick.

ABOUT THE AUTHOR

Thomas Taylor (1758 -- 1835) was an English translator and Neoplatonist, the first to translate into English the complete works of Aristotle and of Plato, as well as the Orphic fragments.

Born in London, Taylor was educated at St. Paul's School, and devoted himself to the study of the classics and of mathematics. After first working as a clerk in Lubbock's Bank, he was appointed Assistant Secretary to the Society for the Encouragement of Art (precursor to the Royal Society of Arts), in which capacity he made many influential friends, who furnished the means for publishing his various translations, which besides Plato and Aristotle, include Proclus, Porphyry, Apuleius, Ocellus Lucanus and other Neoplatonists and Pythagoreans. His aim was the translation of all the untranslated writings of the ancient Greek philosophers.

Taylor was an admirer of Hellenism, most especially in the philosophical framework furnished by Plato and the Neoplatonists Proclus and the "most divine" Iamblichus, whose works he translated into English. So enamored was he of the ancients, that he and his wife talked to one another only in classical Greek.

He was also an outspoken voice against corruption in the Christianity of his day, and its shallowness. Taylor was ridiculed and acquired many enemies, but in other quarters he was well received. Among his friends was the eccentric traveler and philosopher John "Walking" Stewart, whose gatherings Taylor was in the habit of attending. The texts that he used had been edited since the 16th century, but were interrupted by lacunae; Taylor's understanding of the Platonists informed his suggested emendations. His translations were influential on William Blake, Percy Bysshe Shelley and William Wordsworth. In American editions they were read by Ralph Waldo Emerson, Bronson Alcott, and Helena Petrovna Blavatsky, the founder of Theosophy.

Taylor also published several original works on philosophy (in particular, the Neoplatonism of Proclus and Iamblichus) and mathematics.

It appears that he and his wife were landlords at Walworth in the late 1770 to a family that included the 18 year old Mary Wollstonecraft; it is not clear whether the future author of *"A Vindication of the Rights of Woman"* actually knew the Taylors, as at that age she left home for a job as a lady's companion. Consideration of Wollstonecraft's 1792 magnum opus, together with Thomas Paine's *"Rights of Man"* inspired Taylor in his *"A Vindication of the Rights of Brutes"*: if men and women have rights, why not animals too?

List of works

Among his translations are:

- *The Mystical Hymns of Orpheus* (1787)
- *Plato* (1804)
- *Aristotle* (1806–12)
- *The Life of Pythagoras by Iamblichus* (1818)
- *Apuleius*
- *Celsus*
- *Iamblichus*
- *Julian*
- *Maximus*
- *Tyrius*
- *Pausanias*
- *Plotinus*
- *Porphyry*, and
- *Proclus*

Among his miscellanies are:

- *A Vindication of the Rights of Brutes* (1792)
- *The Eleusinian and Bacchic Mysteries: a dissertation* (1790). Amsterdam.
- *Theoretic Arithmetic* (1816).

www.ingramcontent.com/pod-product-compliance
Lightning Source LLC
Chambersburg PA
CBHW021805220426
43662CB00006B/194